Learning Jesus Christ Through the Heidelberg Catechism

LEARNING JESUS CHRIST THROUGH THE HEIDELBERG CATECHISM

Karl Barth

Translated by
Shirley C. Guthrie, Jr.

WILLIAM B. EERDMANS PUBLISHING COMPANY
Grand Rapids, Michigan

Printed in the United States of America

Part I was originally published as *Die christliche Lehre nach dem Heidelberger Katechismus* by Evangelischer Verlag A. G., Zollikon-Zürich, 1948.

Part II was originally published as *Einführung in den Heidelberger Katechismus* by EVZ-Verlag, Zürich, 1960.

First American edition published 1964 as *The Heidelberg Catechism for Today* by John Knox Press.

This edition published through special arrangement with EVZ-Verlag and John Knox Press by Wm. B. Eerdmans Publishing Co., 255 Jefferson Ave. SE, Grand Rapids, Mich. 49503.

Scripture quotations are from the Revised Standard Version, copyright 1946 and 1952 by the Division of Christian Education of the National Council of the Churches of Christ in the United States of America.

Library of Congress Cataloging in Publication Data

Barth, Karl, 1886-1968.
  Learning Jesus Christ through the Heidelberg Catechism.

  Translation of two works: Die christliche Lehre nach dem Heidelberger Katechismus and Einführung in den Heidelberger Katechismus.
  Reprint. Originally published: The Heidelberg Catechism for today. Richmond: John Knox Press, c1964.
  Contents: Christian doctrine according to the Heidelberg Catechism — Introduction to the Heidelberg Catechism.
  1. Heidelberg Catechism. 2. Reformed Church — Doctrinal and controversial works. I. Barth, Karl, 1886-1968. Einführung in den Heidelberger Katechismus. English. II. Title.
  BX9428.B313 1981 238'.42 81-12625
  ISBN 0-8028-1893-5 (pbk.)   AACR2

GUILHELMO GOETERS
septuagenario
collegae, amico, fratri

CONTENTS

Foreword

We know in part, and the present work is an uncompleted sketch. Its publication was requested of me, and since the publication last year of *Dogmatik in Grundriss* [*Dogmatics in Out-Line*, 1949] under similar conditions has been well received, I have thought that this work also might be helpful. I bear full responsibility for the summary paragraphs at the beginning of each section in Part I. The text is the revision of shorthand notes which made the best of my unwritten lectures. I had to be so brief in dealing with the third part of the catechism (because the semester came to an end) that only the summary paragraphs are printed here. The attentive reader will see how I intended to explain the Ten Commandments and the Lord's Prayer in the context of the whole.

If I venture to dedicate this fragment to such a learned man as Wilhelm Goeters, it is because of his especially friendly attitude toward these lectures. Nearing his seventieth year, he came early every morning at 7 o'clock (5 o'clock according to Swiss time that summer!), with a swarm of students to the Chemical Institute in the Poppelsdorfer Allee which I haunted like a curious new version of Dr. Faust, surrounded by all kinds of strangely shaped glassware and apparatus. He himself was well suited to this baroque environment. He was not offended but took a sympathetic interest in the certain transformation to which I subjected this venerable old document. And later in many lively conversations I learned from him what he could tell me from his rich treasure of knowledge about the history of the German Reformed

Church. I remind him now that he once told me that there are at least a hundred particular facts from the earliest history of the Heidelberg Catechism which to date are known only to him. I think it worthwhile to ask him while there is time to make them known for the benefit and profit of us all.

Karl Barth
Basel, August 1948

Translator's Preface

Barth's two short studies of the Heidelberg Catechism included in this volume are not new. *Christian Doctrine According to the Heidelberg Catechism (Die christliche Lehre nach dem Heidelberger Katechismus)* is a series of lectures delivered to students at the University of Bonn in 1947. *Introduction to the Heidelberg Catechism (Einführung in den Heidelberger Katechismus)* is a lecture delivered to a group of Swiss teachers of religion in 1938. But it is appropriate that the translation of these lectures should have been first published when we had just celebrated the 400th anniversary of one of the classical documents of the Reformation.

These two works simultaneously serve three purposes. First of all, they introduce a catechism which, although it is one of the most important writings from the side of the Reformation which stemmed from Calvin, is largely unknown even to many English-speaking Protestants who stand in that tradition. We have been nourished primarily by the Westminster standards with their careful statement of the truth of the gospel in an objective, impersonal, abstractly propositional way—in the scholastic style of the seventeenth century. The Heidelberg Catechism does not represent a different theological orientation. It, too, is a "Calvinistic" document. But it is a statement of Christian truth from a different perspective. Here the Reformed Church confesses the good news of Jesus Christ in a joyful, thankful, free, personal way— with the "existential involvement" as well as the concern for theological correctness of the Reformation period itself. Barth has caught this spirit in his commentary. To read it is to become

11

acquainted with a side of Reformed Protestantism which all too often has remained hidden.

Secondly, Barth introduces the catechism in such a way that we are also given a brief, orderly summary of Reformed doctrine. The Heidelberg Catechism is not only a "confession of faith." It is also *theology*—a coherent statement of *what* we believe as well as a confession of what we *believe*. While it is unmistakably Reformed theology we find here, it is not that in a narrow, denominational sense. The Heidelberg Catechism is "ecumenical" in the best sense of the word. It represents the best of the Lutheran as well as of the Calvinistic Reformation. Although it does not pretend that there are no differences among the Reformed and Lutheran and Roman Catholic traditions, and does not hesitate to point them out, it generally is not a polemic *against* anything or anyone but simply a positive statement of what *Christians* (not just "Calvinists") believe. In introducing us to the Heidelberg Catechism, Barth at the same time thus gives us a systematic introduction to *Christian* theology from a *Reformed* point of view.

Finally, the two works before us also introduce us to the theology of the man who as much as any man is responsible for the renewal of the church and its theology in our own time. Barth expresses here his loyalty to the genuinely Reformed tradition just when at various points he quite openly says that, listening to the same Scriptures which guided our fathers who composed the Heidelberg Catechism, we must say things differently in the twentieth century. Barth lets the catechism speak for itself. He listens to it sympathetically and tries to understand its best intentions even when he thinks we cannot follow it at this or that particular point. But he also takes seriously the catechism's own respect for the authority of Scripture over tradition, and he can therefore criticize and suggest alternatives when he thinks it necessary. This "respectful but free" conversation with the writers of the catechism means that we become acquainted here with the twentieth-century Reformed theologian Karl Barth as well as with the sixteenth-century Reformed theologians Ursinus and Olevianus.

Although both the works included in this volume are expositions of the same document, their approach is different, so that the second supplements rather than simply repeats the first. The first is a question-by-question interpretation and commentary and evaluation of the catechism. The second treats three central themes which run through the whole. Together they give us a view both of the individual trees and of the forest.

Various English versions of the Heidelberg Catechism are available. The present volume uses the 400th anniversary edition translated by Allen O. Miller and M. Eugene Osterhaven (Philadelphia: United Church Press, 1962). Minor variations in translation occasionally occur when they seem to clarify Barth's exposition of the German text.

Except in places where Barth's interpretation of the Greek New Testament is different (Rom. 1:17, for example), biblical quotations are from the Revised Standard Version.

Shirley C. Guthrie, Jr.
Columbia Theological Seminary

Christian Doctrine According to the Heidelberg Catechism

I

Lectures given at the University of Bonn, Summer Semester, 1947.

1 / The Task

Christian doctrine is the attempt, undertaken as a responsibility of the church, to summarize the gospel of Jesus Christ as the content of the church's preaching. Its source and its goal is the authentic witness to the gospel in Holy Scripture. We follow the guidance of the Heidelberg Catechism with the free respect and thankfulness which we owe to a good confession of the fathers of the evangelical church.

---

1. The theme of this series of lectures is usually called "dogmatics." We say here "Christian doctrine" (it being always good in theology to change the concepts occasionally), and mean the same thing. The subject and content of Christian doctrine is the gospel of Jesus Christ. Gospel means *good news*, and Jesus Christ is a name which points to a *person*. This double character of the subject of Christian doctrine distinguishes it from the description of an idea, a truth or system of truths, a world view or philosophy, and also from the description of a rule of life or social order. Christian doctrine does not have to do with any such production of the human spirit or human conscience. It has to do rather with a given message which comes to man and touches him —with an announcement. It has to do with the communication of something new, something which transfers man into a quite

different, completely new and unexpected situation; something which opens up new possibilities to him and leads him into a critical debate with himself and his environment and above all with the one who is the subject of this message or report. For the gospel concerns a person—*this* person, Jesus Christ. It is the existence, being, and work of this person which has such revolutionary, radical, life-invading significance for the man to whom this message is brought.

But gospel does not mean simply news; it means *good* news. Quite apart from whether the fact is known or not, the gospel is objectively glad tidings for every man, for all men in all areas and times. When the gospel is rightly understood and proclaimed, it is gladly proclaimed. And when it is rightly heard, it is gladly heard. For the great new thing which thereby comes into the life of man is joy, help, comfort. "Depart, you sad spirits, for Christ the master of joy comes in." When the gospel is not joyfully spoken and heard as glad tidings, it is not the gospel of Jesus Christ.

Christian doctrine is the *attempt* to summarize the gospel of Jesus Christ. In itself the gospel is boundless, eternal, and therefore inexhaustible. No attempt of Christian doctrine can reproduce it in its fullness. Christian doctrine can thus always be only the summary of various basic lines of thought and main points. This series of lectures also intends to be such an attempt, in full awareness of the fact that we can achieve only from a distance a view of the richness of the subject of Christian doctrine. Christian doctrine is an attempt not only because it is quantitatively impossible to grasp the fullness of the gospel, but above all because the gospel of Jesus Christ is concerned with God's own Word and work, and therefore is something perfect in itself. Measured by it, every human description can only be imperfect, dependent on the condition of the individual's and the church's knowledge from time to time. Nevertheless this attempt *must* be undertaken, and it *may* be undertaken ever afresh. The question arises here whether there is anything like *progress* in these different human attempts and thus in the different forms and kinds of Christian doctrine. This question can be answered neither positively nor negatively. It is a matter for God to decide whether for two thousand years the history of dogma and theology has gone forward or whether Christianity has moved in a circle. We must not concern ourselves with the question whether we move on a historically ascending or descending line. Without any historical romanticism, we are called in our place in history to undertake faithfully this attempt at Christian doctrine, this attempt at a coherent presentation of the gospel of Jesus Christ.

We undertake this attempt as a *responsibility of the church,* that is, not only as the responsibility to give a historical exposition, but as the responsibility of those who are themselves willing and ready to take a stand for what they have heard, making it their own concern; who therefore have not only heard the good news, but have accepted it as news which concerns and touches *them.* It is the responsibility, in other words, of those who find themselves in the community of the church which is founded on the good news of Jesus Christ and to which is entrusted its interpretation and transmission. Christian doctrine is concerned with the task and mission which is entrusted to the church. The church, the Christian community, is as a human community given the honor to proclaim and spread the good news of Jesus Christ in the world. For the sake of this task there is ever a fresh need for Christian doctrine, for such a summary in which the church answers to itself for what it has to say and proclaim. Now the good news of Jesus Christ is not a dead commodity handed over to us so that we can "have" it. Beware of this capitalistic conception of Christianity in any form, old or new! The gospel must ever again be explored and sought and inquired into. It demands work, reflection, exertion. It demands faithfulness and independent investigation. The church may not avoid this effort, for its existence as church depends upon it. Doctrine is thus not its own goal. One can work at theology for theology's sake just as little as he can work at art for art's sake. Christian doctrine is rather a part of the service of the community, service to God and to neighbor. It is thus a part of the church's liturgy. In this sense we will do our work, and in this sense only can it be done. When we teach or study theology, we stand in the service of the church.

2. But also with regard to its knowledge, Christian doctrine does not depend upon itself. It has a *source* and a *goal*. The place from which it comes and the place toward which it moves is distinguished also formally from every theoretical statement or idea or world view. Above all Christian doctrine towers a form of Christian doctrine which is distinguished from all other forms as the original form: the *authentic,* original, and therefore normative *witness of the gospel* to Jesus Christ as it is given in the Scriptures of the Old and New Testaments. Jesus Christ is the one whom the prophets and apostles saw and heard and touched as the content of the good news. In this concrete form he is the criterion of the church's proclamation. Therefore Christian doctrine must come from this concrete form, from *exegesis*. And it must lead to better exegesis, to clearer visibleness of this concrete form. It can be a meaningful undertaking only in this double connection. Christian doctrine which wanted to cut itself off from exegesis would be indistinguishable from human speculation and therefore unfit for service in the church. Beware of every pursuit of theology which neglects the original task of theology, exegesis, that serious and difficult task to which also the knowledge of Greek and Hebrew belongs!

3. Finally, there is no *absolute method* of Christian doctrine. There have always been different paths in this work, and which path is taken is less important than how it is pursued. The main rule, that all Christian doctrine must be grounded on and lead to Scripture, must of course be enforced under all circumstances. To this may be added the first secondary rule: Good (i.e., right) Christian doctrine does not take place in a vacuum of solitary thinking; it chooses its place in the fellowship of the saints, in connection with the living, thinking, and knowing of the whole Christian church, not only in the present but also in the past. Right Christian doctrine thus stands necessarily in connection with the teaching of the *fathers* who have also worked at this same task. Christian doctrine does not will to be an original undertaking; it places itself in a line. This can be methodologically expressed by the fact that we follow one of the writings of the fathers. When we do that, we have to consider *who* we follow.

There are more and less trustworthy fathers in the Christian church. We may risk the assertion that in the *Heidelberg Catechism* we have a good confession of the Reformed church which was grounded on and renewed by the gospel.

"Christian Doctrine According to the Heidelberg Catechism" is the title of this series of lectures.

"According to the Heidelberg Catechism" does not mean that we shall give a *historical exegesis* of the catechism. We shall give careful attention to the text and follow it from question to question in order to understand it in detail. We cannot avoid a strict study of this little book. But our task is not the history of dogma; it is dogmatics. We are primarily interested in Christian doctrine as such and not in the Heidelberg Catechism.

Further, the title does not mean that we shall present *Heidelberg orthodoxy*. This catechism also was an attempt at Christian doctrine. We live no longer in the sixteenth but in the twentieth century. This simple fact must be emphasized especially here in Germany today. If we concern ourselves *today* with Christian doctrine, there is no point in staring spellbound at the sixteenth century and holding on to what was said then and there as unmoveably and unchangeably as possible. Such a procedure would be inconsistent with the Reformation. It is always a misunderstanding of the communion of saints and a misunderstanding also of the fathers when their confession is later understood as chains, so that Christian doctrine today could only be a repetition of their confession. In the communion of the saints there should be *reverence* and *thankfulness* for the fathers of the church, those who have gone before us and in their time have reflected on the gospel. But there is also *freedom* in the communion of the saints. Real respect and real thanksgiving are free. Both are called for in relation to the Heidelberg Catechism. To exercise both in relation to it is the purpose of this series of lectures. In general we will follow the direction of the catechism, but we will allow ourselves deviations when it seems necessary. Even in such deviations we will agree with what the Heidelberg Catechism really intended. Not to allow and require such freedom would mean that we in the church had returned to a kind of tradition which stands with equal honor alongside Holy Scripture. The catechism points to the Holy Scriptures and it also may and must be measured by them. It is the furthest thing from my mind in these lectures to pour oil on the fire of the *confessionalism* which unfortunately lives again in Germany. I consider this confessionalism one of the most questionable things which is happening today in German theology and in the German church.

2 / *The Heidelberg Catechism*

The Heidelberg Catechism originated in connection with the regulation of the order of common worship as the form of Christian doctrine in which one of the churches which was renewed in the sixteenth century expressed its knowledge of the gospel in a way characteristic of the positive direction of the whole Reformation.

The confessional writing with which we are now concerned is interesting because, more clearly than all other confessions of Lutheran or Reformed origin, it grew out of the immediate necessities of life of a *church*. Unlike some other confessional writings, the Heidelberg Catechism in origin and ruling intention is not a piece of abstract theology, abstract polemics, or church politics; it is an element of the life of the church.

On November 15, 1563, the Elector Frederick III of the Palatinate made public and put into effect a church order for his land. 1563 was no longer the time of the beginning of the Reformation and its first battles, but the time of the beginning Counter-Reformation, of the stabilization of the renewed churches, of the wearisome and difficult debate between the Lutherans and Calvinists. All this made it desirable and necessary for the church to take a stand on a firm foundation in order to protect itself against the many different tendencies and movements which broke out everywhere. With this church order of 1563, the Elector from the Palatinate wanted in his capacity as *praecipuum membrum ecclesiae* (first member of the church) to provide for the unity of the church and above all of church worship. The so-called Heidelberg or Palatine Catechism belongs in the framework of this church order. It is the integrating part of the *liturgy*, placed between the formulas for baptism and the Lord's Supper—on the way, so to speak, between the grace which has already been shown and the grace yet to be shown. Here, between foundation and eschaton, the question is asked concerning the Christian life, concerning "the only comfort in life and in death." The Palatine church order expressed itself explicitly on the practical intention of this particular undertaking. It makes four points: (1) The catechism should serve the instruction of youth; (2) it should serve the instruction of pastors and teachers; (3) it should be used in public worship, specifically in nine selections which were to be read, one each Sunday, in nine Sunday cycles; (4) it should be divided into 52 Sundays and used not as the basic text but as the basic theme for the afternoon worship service or sermon.

The catechism is not the work of one author; it is the work of a *community*. The church order says expressly that "our most distinguished theologians, superintendents, church servants, and other godly learned men" worked on it. As Olevianus wrote to Bullinger, *it is a collection of the pious thoughts not of one but of many*. We have a text, therefore, which came out of the church community. Nevertheless, *two theologians* had a decisive part in this work. The first was *Caspar Olevianus*, who was born in Treves in 1536. In 1559 he was active there as a reformer and was expelled. After 1560 he was first professor and then pastor in Heidelberg. In 1562 and 1563 he helped in the working out of the church order. He was expelled from the Palatinate in 1576 with the coming of the Lutheran reaction. He died in 1587. The second author was *Zacharias Ursinus*, who was born in Breslau in 1534. He studied with Melanchthon, Calvin, and Bullinger, and in 1562 became professor in Heidelberg. He also was banished in 1576. He died in 1587. Ursinus was 28 years old and Olevianus 26 when the catechism was composed.

There were certain important *earlier texts* which preceded this work. The catechism of Leo Jud appeared in 1541; and the catechism of the German church in London, composed by Marten Micronius, appeared in 1559. But of decisive importance was Calvin's catechism of 1542, which lay before Olevianus and Ursinus as they worked. This catechism differs from the Lutheran confession at an important point: It places the credo and the sacraments before the law. Ursinus himself had already earlier attempted catechetical theological work. He had published a *Summa theologiae* and a *Catechismus minor* in which we already find the outline *miseria-liberatio-gratitudo* [misery-redemption-gratitude]. But this threefold division is not an original invention of Ursinus. It goes back to a little work which appeared in 1547, "A Short Orderly Summary of the Right True Teaching of Our Faith," composed by an unknown "good-hearted man," published by a *Lutheran!* In 1558 this work was reprinted in Heidelberg. Ursinus certainly contributed decisively to the systematic work of the new catechism. In his work also the summary of the law and of prayer is seen from the point of view of *gratitude*. The first question comes from him also: "What is your only comfort in life and in death?" Olevianus' participation seems essentially to have consisted in linguistic revision and formulation.

The *material* of the catechism was presented in the five traditional parts which control also the Lutheran catechism: confession of faith, the two sacraments, the law, and the Lord's Prayer.

The Heidelberg Catechism, introduced in the Palatinate, has become known also in wide circles in the rest of the Protestant world. It was for centuries, and to some extent still remains, the manual and textbook of German, Dutch, Hungarian, and Swiss Reformed Christians. Yet peculiarly Reformed doctrines play only a small part in this catechism. They are essentially limited to questions 47-48 (the way in which Christ is omnipresent), question 72 on baptism (the way in which water is related to the washing away of sins), questions 75-79 on the Lord's Supper (the way in which the body and blood of Christ are really present in the elements). These are the only three points which can be called *exclusively* Reformed doctrine. The doctrine of predestination, a point which strongly stirred Reformed Christians in the sixteenth century, is mentioned only marginally here, and the dangers feared in view of it also remain invisible. There is serious opposition in the catechism to the theory and practice of the Roman Catholic Church. At this point the lines are clearly drawn and the "no" is unmistakable.

The Heidelberg Catechism is a document which expresses a *general evangelical comprehension.* Apart from the three points mentioned above, a reasonable Lutheranism should also be able to stand on this ground. The catechism is not a different but only a differently formulated confession of the one evangelical faith. Scholastic nuances are present which at that time were frightening, but they in no way justify our drawing up the old battle lines again today, much less our giving such nuances a church-dividing significance. The catechism points to the *positive* significance of the Reformation. This makes it usable as the foundation for a development of Christian doctrine.

Now we shall briefly summarize the substance of the Reformed confession as contained in the Heidelberg Catechism.

1. The catechism contains a particular concept of *God.* It speaks of God as one different from all creatures; he stands free and superior over against man. This majesty of God, and the corresponding reverence of man before him, is the first characteristic of this theology. It is important to emphasize this, because the catechism, as the outline itself indicates, is oriented soteriologically and thus is interested in the salvation of man. One may say that it is distinctively a theology of the third article, a theology of the Holy Spirit, constructed from the particular point of view of the work of God in relation to man. A theology so oriented stands in danger of anthropocentricity, that is, of slipping into a one-sided interest in man so that God and the things of God become only an exponent of human experience. The Heidelberg Catechism has often been reproached for a certain tendency in this direction. Is it a forerunner of Schleiermacher? We would do well not to overlook the background of its concept of God. The grace of God in relation to man is and remains free grace.

The catechism speaks powerfully of the fact that God is for man —but we may not forget on the other hand how man appears there first as man who is claimed for God.

2. In this text God is no *Deus nudus, absolutus, absconditus* ["naked," absolute, hidden God]. When the word "God" appears, it always refers to *God in Jesus Christ* (q. 26!). In the words of an often-repeated expression, God is "he who has revealed himself in his Word" (qq. 25, 95, 117). In Barmen in 1934, the evangelical church summarized its faith with the words: "Jesus Christ, as he is testified to us in Holy Scripture, is the one Word of God, whom we are to hear, and whom we are to trust and obey in life and in death." This first paragraph of the Barmen Declaration was not just formally stated in agreement with question 1 of the Heidelberg Catechism. A theology which is not grounded in the Word of God in Jesus Christ cannot in any case appeal to this catechism.

3. When the Heidelberg Catechism speaks of Jesus Christ, it means thereby to include all God's *kindness,* that is, the one full salvation for men, the assurance of forgiveness and the claim on our lives, our liberation to service (cf. Barmen, II). At this point we must of course make a correction. The catechism has a tendency to limit this kindness of God to Christendom or to the church. A somewhat narrow and slightly egotistical understanding of the church and of Christianity can be detected here. We find ourselves within the walls of the church, in the circle of the pious, and the evil world unfortunately has no part in this affair. But the name of God, his kingdom and his will, reach beyond the church and over its walls. "God so loved the *world.*" "You are the light of the *world.*" That is the note which must be sounded in genuinely evangelical doctrine! According to Holy Scripture, the goal of Christianity and the church is not Christianity and the church, but service in God's work and therefore also service of men. The church is the place where God is praised in such a way that others are called. We do not fundamentally disagree with the catechism if we emphasize this. It also says that the concern of Christians is not that we should go to heaven but that God should be praised through us (qq. 86, 99, 122). Ques-

tion 128 says: ". . . that not we ourselves, but thy holy name may be glorified forever." And question 86: ". . . that we . . . may win our neighbors to Christ." On question 1, 1 John 2:2 is cited: "He is the expiation for our sins, and not for ours only but also for the sins of the whole world." And on question 2, 1 Peter 2:9: "But you are a chosen race, a royal priesthood, a holy nation, God's own people, that you may declare the wonderful deeds of him who called you out of darkness into his marvelous light." Also on question 2, Luke 24:48: "You are witnesses of these things."

4. The Heidelberg Catechism specifically follows the theology of the Reformation in calling man's reception of God's kindness, thus the way this kindness is appropriated by man, *faith*. A man who says yes to the fact that God in Jesus Christ is for us is one who *believes*. And as a believer he will never understand himself other than as a part of God's kindness: he *may* believe. All his achievements could not help him to receive God's kindness. "Works" cannot "justify" him. Thus the freedom for grace is grounded in the freedom of the gracious God.

5. But faith means precisely man's *freedom to action*. *Charis* (grace) is the foundation of man's *eucharistia* (thankfulness) and summons it as a call summons an echo. According to the Heidelberg Catechism, there is no conflict between the majesty of God and the hard work of man. Martin Luther also surely had this connection between faith and work in mind, but we may say that this connection never became so clear and transparent with him. When one reads Luther's expositions on gospel and law, one gets the slight impression of a parade in which one takes one step forward and two steps backward. Calvin and his followers are definitely less ambiguous in their theological exposition at this point, and in a document such as the Heidelberg Catechism we receive clearer guidance on the relation between dogmatics and ethics.

6. The place where divine and human freedom meet is in the *community*. I speak deliberately of community rather than church, and mean thereby Christians in their fellowship with Christ and in their fellowship of faith with one another, without the interposition of an "office." To this community is entrusted *service* of the gospel. For the gospel is spoken to the community—the whole

community. God's name is to be praised through the service of the community, through the communion of the saints, and not through the special service of theologians and priests.

7. But all this clearly stands in the Heidelberg Catechism under the sign of a "not yet," that is, under the sign of the still outstanding final revelation. Question 1 says, "What is your only comfort in life and in death?" *Comfort* points to the fact that it has not yet appeared what we shall be. We may only go forward to meet our future form; we live now in *expectancy* of this future revelation.

These are the seven nails which are driven home in the Heidelberg Catechism. We have here the common property of the whole Reformation. What significance can the differences among the evangelical confessions have beside these seven basic truths? Is it not a waste of time and energy to stick obstinately to these differences instead of concentrating on the great common truth which was commonly recognized again in the Reformation?

3 / The Only Comfort

(QUESTIONS 1-2)

The gospel is the good news entrusted to the Christian community that sinful, and therefore lost, man, in the tribulation of his death and of his life overshadowed by death, belongs to Jesus Christ. Through Christ, complete order has been created between God and this man, and through Christ he is made completely certain of his future and completely joyful in obedience. To life in this comfort there belongs with equal necessity the recognition of man's guilty need, his undeserved preservation, his free servitude.

The first and second questions of the Heidelberg Catechism stand under the sign of the word "comfort." Comfort means generally a provisional but effective and promising help given to man in a difficult situation. It is help which becomes good reason, despite the fact that he has serious and even urgent reasons to the contrary, *nevertheless* to endure, *nevertheless* to take courage, *nevertheless* to be joyful. When one really comforts another, he offers him help which becomes the ground for such a "nevertheless." When one lets himself be comforted, he accepts this help; he lets himself be given this ground. Comfort in this sense is the content of the gospel. And for this reason the gospel is *good* news.

In order to understand this, it is necessary to know what the difficult situation is in which the man finds himself who needs comfort and has reason nevertheless to endure, nevertheless to take courage, nevertheless to be patient and joyful.

The Heidelberg Catechism describes this difficult situation of man quite simply with the words *life and death,* the emphasis obviously falling on the latter. Human life has an eschatological edge, a boundary line. Man is destined one day to die. At this boundary line falls the decision about his existence, a decision which means being or non-being. And that is what makes the situation of man so difficult, so needful of comfort: he is threatened by non-being. Man must expect at the end a *Judge* whom he must absolutely fear (q. 52). He must expect at the boundary line in his death a *total destruction* of his being, soul and body (q. 57). And finally he must expect after this judgment and after this total destruction *everlasting death* (q. 58). The life of man stands under this shadow. It is on the way to death. And this is the *tribulation* in which the gospel comforts man and therefore gives him reason nevertheless to endure, nevertheless to take courage, nevertheless to be joyful. Question 1 unfolds this comfort *in nuce* and attempts to say in a paragraph what the comfort is which can do this. Question 2 describes the three elements of the knowledge indispensable to life and death in this comfort.

Question 1. **What is your only comfort, in life and in death?** That I belong—body and soul, in life and in death—not to myself but to my faithful Savior, Jesus Christ, who at the cost of his own blood has fully paid for all my sins and has completely freed me from the dominion of the devil; that he protects me so well that without the will of my Father in heaven not a hair can fall from my head; indeed, that everything must fit his purpose for my salvation. Therefore, by his Holy Spirit, he also assures me of eternal life, and makes me wholeheartedly willing and ready from now on to live for him.

The decisive phrase in this long statement is: *I belong to Jesus Christ.* Everything else is only an explication of these five words. The only thing to be said of man is that he belongs totally to Jesus Christ, body and soul, in life and in death. He belongs to Jesus Christ without limit and without reservation. We have here *complete* comfort for the *whole* man. Anything else which may be said relevantly follows simply from the being and work of the subject Jesus Christ who owns man. Creation (q. 26) and church (q. 54) also will be explained in a corresponding way.

This in itself explains why and in what sense this comfort is called the *only* comfort. The ground of our salvation is the *one* Jesus Christ (qq. 29-30). We have only *one* "bringer of salvation." This also explains the liveliness with which questions 61, 66-67, and especially 80 speak of the *one* sacrifice and the *one* satisfaction; and the emphasis with which the church speaks of *one* true God (qq. 25, 94, 95, 117). (We must distinguish Christian monotheism very clearly from that of Islam! The former means the *one Jesus Christ.*) But on this basis it also becomes clear that the *need* of man is *one single* need for which there can only be one single comfort.

I belong not to myself but to Jesus Christ. I am not my own lord and not my own property. Therefore also anxiety about myself—anxiety is the comprehensive expression for the existence of a comfortless man—is not my affair. "Do you not know that . . . you are not your own" (1 Cor. 6:19). "I belong to my faithful Savior, Jesus Christ." That means: I exist eccentrically; I belong to this Other. I belong to this Lord completely, with my anxiety and my misery, but also with my successes and my achievements. He is my Counsel, my Helper, my Defender. He is this because he has redeemed and "bought us for his very own" (q. 34).

The concept, *apolytrosis,* redemption, stands out clearly here. We are "incorporated into him" (q. 20). We "share" in him (q. 32). We are "united . . . to his blessed body" (q. 76), "ingrafted" into him (q. 64). This is the exposition of the view of the New Testament as seen for instance in Romans 14:7 f.: "None of us lives to himself, and none of us dies to himself. If we live, we live to the Lord, and if we die, we die to the Lord; so then, whether we live or whether we die, we are the Lord's." Or 1 Corinthians 3:23: "And you are Christ's. . . ." The content of all comfort is that this is true. I am his.

Two groups of statements follow from this:

> (a) ". . . who at the cost of his own *blood* has fully paid for all my sins, and has completely freed me from the dominion of the devil. . . ."
>
> (b) "Therefore, by his *Holy Spirit,* he also assures me of eternal life, and makes me wholeheartedly willing and ready from now on to live for him."

The first group of statements is dominated by the concept "his own blood" and the second group by the concept "his Holy Spirit." This contrast is a scheme which will appear often in the catechism (cf. qq. 69-74, 86). Blood and Spirit make him Comforter and as such the comfort of my life and death. We are concerned here with his *objective action for us* and his *subjective action on us and in us.* The comfort of the gospel consists in the fact that it speaks of both, of the *totality* of the person and of the work of Jesus Christ.

1. The *objective reason* in tribulation nevertheless to endure, nevertheless to take courage, nevertheless to be joyful, is that in his blood (i.e., in giving up his life) Jesus Christ has restored the confused order between God and man. Our tribulation consists objectively in the fact that this order is destroyed and the peace between God and man broken. Man is a *sinner.* He has become the offender and enemy of God.

But as sinner, man is *lost,* a prisoner of death. God will not be mocked. Sinful man falls into the power of Satan, into the hands of a *foreign* power in which his life is not well protected. He stumbles into the sphere of the anti-divine and therefore also of the anti-human. In Jesus Christ also this violated right of man is restored, for he has *freed* us from this power. Man is thereby placed again in a position in which he may and therefore also can live. He is thus *protected* and preserved, placed in a position of freedom, so that "without the will of my Father in heaven not a hair can fall from my head; indeed, that everything must fit his purpose for my salvation." That is the right of man which is now again honored, so that objectively he may exist as one fully protected. "And this is the will of him who sent me, that I should lose nothing of all that he has given me . . ." (John 6:39). "We know that in everything God works for good with those who love him . . ." (Rom. 8:28).

2. Alongside this objective reason for our comfort stands the *subjective reason* in tribulation nevertheless to endure, nevertheless to take courage, nevertheless to be joyful: *his Holy Spirit.* The Holy Spirit is God himself working and giving evidence in us. He transfers man into the freedom of the order restored by Jesus Christ. "In him you also . . . were sealed with the promised Holy Spirit . . ." (Eph. 1:13).

(a) By his Holy Spirit, Jesus Christ assures me of *eternal life.* Sinful man lives in anxiety and in anxiety sees his future as a most severely threatened future. The man who exists in destroyed order lives in worry about what is going to happen. What is going to happen is—death. This shadow lies over our life and makes the dawn of every new day full of anxiety. In Jesus Christ the destroyed order, the shattered right of man, is again established. Man is thereby put in a position in which he can and may live. He is therefore protected, guarded, defended, transferred to a situation of freedom, so that "without the will of my Father in heaven not a hair can fall from my head; indeed, that everything must fit his purpose for my salvation." That is the right of man which now is again honored.

Therefore the appearance of human life, the anxiety in which man exists, is not only alleviated but totally changed. Because Jesus Christ by his Holy Spirit assures me of eternal life, my life in time may also stand under this assurance. The "radiant morning of eternity, the light of inexhaustible light," may announce itself in the temporal morning light of every day of my life. The command, "Do not be anxious about tomorrow," has become unnecessary. "In him you were sealed with the promised Holy Spirit." That is valid now, finally valid.

(b) ". . . and makes me wholeheartedly willing and ready from now on to live for him." Through the Holy Spirit there comes a very simple but very clear *direction* in the life of man. He makes me willing and ready. That does not mean that he makes me into a saint or a hero. The Heidelberg Catechism uses no grandiose words. It speaks with clarity and at the same time with restraint. The distinguishing mark of the new man made alive by the Holy Spirit is "complete joy in God through Christ and a strong desire to live according to the will of God in all good works" (q. 90). Question 114 speaks of a "serious purpose" and question 115 says even more reservedly that "we earnestly seek. . . ." The modesty of expression and the decisiveness of the fact—we must see both things here. "For all who are led by the Spirit of God are sons of God" (Rom. 8:14). That is the work of Jesus Christ, our comfort in life and death, the content of the gospel.

Question 2. **How many things must you know that you may live and die in the blessedness of this comfort?** Three. First, the greatness of my sin and wretchedness. Second, how I am freed from all my sins and their wretched consequences. Third, what gratitude I owe to God for such redemption.

This question clarifies the meaning, purpose, and plan of *Christian doctrine* as the authors of the Heidelberg Catechism saw it. In order to receive the one comfort and to be able to live and die by it, a definite *knowledge* is necessary. This comfort wants to be understood; it is therefore addressed also to the reason. Vast and mysterious as it is, it is not irrational. There is something to *perceive* and thus also something to *know*. And this not only for a few learned theologians or for a few men with a special intellectual inclination, but for everyone. The catechism is unequivocal also in this respect. According to question 6, man was created "so that he might rightly *know* God his Creator." We must "learn" the Word of God (q. 103). Faith is "a certain *knowledge* by which I accept as true all that God has revealed to us in his Word . . ." (q. 21): To hallow the name of God means first of all "to *know* thee rightly" (q. 122). According to the catechism (and Rom. 12:1), life in comfort is thus a *logike latreia,* a reasonable service, just as surely as this comfort of the gospel is the comfort of God. Where God is, there is also wisdom, and on man's side accordingly a perceiving and knowing. This comfort is addressed to the *whole* man—also the knowing man.

Question 2 outlines the plan of Christian teaching. It would not be impossible to develop such an outline on the basis of question 1, but the catechism does not choose this way. It indicates three lines upon which it will build: man by his own guilt is in *need;* without merit he is *preserved;* he stands therefore in free *servitude.* "For we ourselves were once foolish, disobedient, led astray, slaves to various passions and pleasures, passing our days in malice and envy, hated by men and hating one another; but when the goodness and loving kindness of God our Savior appeared, he saved us, not because of deeds done by us in righteousness, but in virtue of his own mercy, by the washing of regeneration and renewal in the Holy Spirit, which he poured out upon us richly through Jesus Christ our Savior, so that we might be justified by his grace and become heirs in hope of eternal life" (Titus 3:3-7). "It is written, that the Christ should suffer and on the third day rise from the dead, and that repentance and forgiveness of sins should be preached in his name to all nations, beginning from Jerusalem. You are witnesses of these things" (Luke 24:46-48). Misery, exhortation, thankfulness—all three are included in *comfort.*

4 / *God's Indictment*

(QUESTIONS 3-9)

Because Jesus Christ has loved God above all else and his neighbor as himself, it is revealed in him that, without reason and excuse, from birth through his whole life, man does the opposite and thus violates the right of God. But it is already comfort that it is precisely Jesus Christ who brings this indictment against man.

Part I: "Man's Sin and Guilt." We notice first of all quite generally how much shorter this part is than the two following parts. That is not accidental or immaterial. "For his anger is but for a moment, and his favor is for a lifetime" (Ps. 30:5). "In overflowing wrath for a moment I hid my face from you, but with everlasting love I will have compassion on you, says the LORD, your Redeemer" (Isa. 54:8). As we have already seen, what we hear in questions 3-9 and 10-11 is included under *comfort*. The content of these questions is not drawn from a different, foreign source but from the one Christian truth, and therefore it must not be abstractly developed. Precisely the Christian man, the believing man, will always be man as he is described here. This is the starting point of the man who has to do with Jesus Christ. The man who will perceive this truth is not the unbelieving man, man before his new birth, but the man to whom the good news has come and who has experienced grace. *He* knows about human wretchedness. The decisive No to this man as it is expressed in questions 5, 6, and 9 is only possible in that final court of appeal in which it can by no means be the last word. For from the point of view of the gospel, man is never seen as he is in himself, but always as the property of his faithful Savior.

Question 3. **Where do you learn of your sin and its wretched consequences?** From the Law of God.

Question 4. **What does the Law of God require of us?** Jesus Christ teaches this in a summary in Matthew 22:37-40: You shall love the Lord your God with all your heart, and with all your soul, and with all your mind. This is the first and great commandment. And a second is like it, you shall love your neighbor as yourself. On these two commandments depend all the law and the prophets.

Questions 3-9 speak of an indictment under which man stands. God's Word accuses him of violating and destroying the right, the order, which was established between himself and God. That is the reason for his misery. Just those who know of the Word of God, who are willing and ready to hear it, and who hold to the one comfort in life and in death—just they know also that they are those who violate the right of God (q. 60). *They* are those who are accused by their consciences, who know that "even our best works in this life are all imperfect and defiled with sin" (q. 62), who know that "we increase our debt each day" (q. 13). *They* know that "even the holiest of them make only a small beginning in obedience in this life" (q. 114), that "evil . . . clings to us" (q. 126), and therefore that only those should come to the table of the Lord "who are displeased with themselves for their sins" (q. 81).

Question 5. **Can you keep all this perfectly?** No, for by nature I am prone to hate God and my neighbor.

It is not even open to question whether man can perfectly keep the right established by God's law. He is inwardly and radically the transgressor of that law, "prone to hate God and . . . neighbor."

Question 6. **Did God create man evil and perverse like this?** No. On the contrary, God created man good and in his image, that is, in true righteousness and holiness, so that he might rightly know God his Creator, love him with his whole heart, and live with him in eternal blessedness, praising and glorifying him.

Man's sinfulness does not come from God's creation. God created man good (Gen. 1:31), "so that he might rightly know God his Creator, love him with his whole heart, and live with him in eternal blessedness, praising and glorifying him." That is the divine right of the *covenant* in which man has his ground of existence.

Question 7. **Where, then, does this corruption of human nature come from?** From the fall and disobedience of our first parents, Adam and Eve, in the Garden of Eden; whereby our human life is so poisoned that we are all conceived and born in the state of sin.

Man's becoming a law-breaker is the result of his *fall* from the covenant, of the disobedience with which he entered history and placed himself in the impossible situation of sin.

Question 8. **But are we so perverted that we are altogether unable to do good and prone to do evil?** Yes, unless we are born again through the Spirit of God.

Therefore man now appears in all the individuals of humanity as incapable of any good and prone to all evil. He needs a "new beginning" if it is to be otherwise.

Question 9. **Is not God unjust in requiring of man in his Law what he cannot do?** No, for God so created man that he could do it. But man, upon the instigation of the devil, by deliberate disobedience, has cheated himself and all his descendants out of these gifts.

Man cannot go forward. He stands under a historical power and can do nothing about it. God created him good, but man has renounced and lost his freedom.

It is noteworthy that in this whole context we find no reflection (such as later would have been introduced here) on the particular misdeeds of man. Already in the sixteenth century, man was no angel, and it would have been easy to call his misdeeds by name. But it is only said that he is incapable of any good and prone to hate God and his neighbor. Who has ears to hear, let him hear!

Further, nothing is said in this context of various good and favorable things about man which might perhaps also have been mentioned. The fact that man is evil remains, and cannot be explained even by some philosophy of history.

Where does the authority and truth of this indictment come from? Certainly not from the impressions of man one can gain from time to time. These impressions change. It is clearer today than thirty or forty years ago that man is *not* "basically" good, that the whitewash of humanism and culture is painfully thin and that not much is needed for it to crumble away and expose a subhuman, brutal being. But we must be clear that this contemporary point of view, too, can change again. During the Thirty Years' War everyone was convinced that man is not good and that he therefore is justly accused. This war came to an end in 1648, and before the end of the same century, Leibniz began to form a school with his optimistic teachings and to anticipate the eighteenth century with its glowing view of man's benevolence and virtue. Roman Catholics and humanists are thus one in the opinion that it is an exaggeration to characterize man as incapable of any good and by nature prone to hate God and neighbor.

But the indictment of which the catechism speaks does not come from various debatable points of view and impressions. It has quite different grounds. It is not just a human indictment. The statements in questions 3-9 spring neither from optimism nor pessimism, but from listening to the law of God. Everything depends upon whether both the more indulgent evaluation of man and our presently more severe view stand in this confrontation. And in this confrontation the decision is made: Man is evil. "We were by nature children of wrath . . ." (Eph. 2:3). "None is righteous, no, not one" (Rom. 3:10). "Every imagination of the thoughts of his heart was only evil continually" (Gen. 6:5). "All have sinned and fall short of the glory of God" (Rom. 3:23). "All we like sheep have gone astray . . ." (Isa. 53:6). "That which is born of the flesh is flesh" (John 3:6). "For the mind that is set on the flesh is hostile to God; it does not submit to God's law, indeed it cannot" (Rom. 8:7). "Man . . . drinks iniquity like water!" (Job 15:16). That is man—not according to some self-evaluation, but according to what God has said to him.

What is this *law of God* which so harshly accuses man? Where and how is it heard? We may not answer too quickly that it is heard in the *conscience,* nor, unfortunately, may we speak too loudly of *natural law.* A general law of nature which we bear within us does not place us under this indictment. Our catechism points us to the divine law in Holy Scriptures. Oh, it speaks of the *Ten Commandments?* Yes, it does do that, but we must remember that these Ten Commandments are the ordinances of the *covenant of grace.* The two tables are valid within in covenant. Here and only here do they show man to be the enemy of God. For what does the man who does not know of God's grace know of his own sin? The Ten Commandments were given to the people of God. They are rules of life for those to whom God has shown his love and grace. The substance of the covenant of grace is Jesus Christ. Therefore, question 5 points to him. Christ not only interpreted and repeated the Old Testament, but he himself was the one who in his person fulfilled the law. He is the one who loved God and man, who restores to God and man their right. Thus "Jesus Christ teaches us this (law) in a summary." In him God stands in the place of man, man stands in the place of God, both in the total sense of question 113. When we speak of the law, we have to do with him—with him as the one who truly and concretely confronts us, in whom also Genesis 1:31 is true. "All things were made through him, and without him was not anything . . ." (John 1:3, Col. 1:16 f., Heb. 1:2). In this context note the citation from Isaiah 53 in question 8: "The Lord has laid on him the iniquity of us all." *He* is our accuser—God's grace in person! Therefore, because it is he, God's indictment is inescapable. Therefore it stands, despite and in the midst of all changing human views and opinions.

But if the indictment expressed in questions 3-9 is valid in the light of Christ and must be understood as the revelation of grace, it can no longer encounter us as an abstract indictment, as a law which kills. It is full of the hidden comfort of the gospel. The one who accuses us is not against us. He is no stranger. Even if we are his enemies, he is not our enemy. His faithfulness has no limits. So already at this point we may anticipate the powerful verdict of question 52: "I may await with head held high the very Judge from heaven who has already submitted himself to the judgment of God for me. . . ." That is no weakening of the indictment in questions 3-9. Everything said against man there holds good. But it is God's love that so burns. Therefore even the painful burning of this indictment, just because it is no self-indictment, stands in the context of 2 Corinthians 3:18: "We all, with unveiled face, beholding the glory of the Lord, are being changed into his likeness from one degree of glory to another; for this comes from the Lord who is the Spirit."

5 / God's Verdict

(QUESTIONS 10-11)

Jesus Christ has suffered in man's place the rejection and condemnation which must follow sin and into which man in himself has hopelessly fallen. Therefore in Christ it is also revealed that by his own fault man's right before God has been lost. But it is already comfort that it is Jesus Christ who declares to him this verdict.

Question 10. **Will God let man get by with such disobedience and defection?** Certainly not, for the wrath of God is revealed from heaven, both against our inborn sinfulness and our actual sins, and he will punish them according to his righteous judgment in time and in eternity, as he has declared: "Cursed be everyone who does not abide by all things written in the book of the Law, and do them."

Question 11. **But is not God also merciful?** God is indeed merciful and gracious, but he is also righteous. It is his righteousness which requires that sin committed against the supreme majesty of God be punished with extreme, that is, with eternal punishment of body and soul.

The indictment developed in questions 3-9 is the indictment of *God.* And because God's indictment is true, it is followed by the *verdict* which declares man guilty and indicates the *penalty* which falls hopelessly upon him. When man violates God's right he forfeits his own right. That is what question 10 says. With his creation, man is given a right, the right as the child of God to exist before and with God. He has forfeited this right by going a way which can only lead him to fall into the depths. The fact that God is good to man, that he is merciful, does not exclude but includes the conclusion that man in himself is lost. This lostness is man's misery. God's goodness would not be mercy if it were not also righteousness. "God is indeed merciful and gracious, but he is also righteous" (q. 11). These two statements belong together: God is merciful *in that* he is righteous. When God's right is violated, man's right also comes to an end. So close and so intimate is the connection between God and man. If God is not to let man's right be violated, then his divine right also must be reestablished. It is true and holds good that death came into the world through sin (Rom. 5:12). "For thou art not a God who delights in wickedness; evil may not sojourn with thee" (Ps. 5:4). God's honor—but also man's salvation—depends on the fact that he cannot tolerate the destruction of his order, that forgiveness therefore cannot mean an overlooking of guilt. This destruction must be exposed as destruction and as such put out of the way. God is "terribly angry." Questions 14, 17, and 37 also speak of the eternal "burden of God's wrath." Sometimes in the Christian church and in Christian theology people have been astonished or even offended at this concept of the wrath of God. Some have even thought that at this point they must correct the Bible, believing that wrath is unworthy of God. Especially Albrecht Ritschl attempted with an artificial exegesis to eliminate this concept.

But that is an impossible undertaking which contradicts the meaning of the gospel. For when Scripture and the Heidelberg Catechism speak of the wrath of God, they want to say thereby that God lives, that he is near and interested in man—so near that man can violate his "supreme majesty." In entering into a covenant of grace with man, God has come so near to man that he is affected by what man is and does, so near that he can be hurt by man. The being and doing of man touch his heart. Understood in this way, the word of God's wrath is full of comfort and gospel, full of good news, even when it is true and holds good that this feeling of God is an overwhelming reaction and a consuming fire. God, who is the Lord of man, resists the enmity of man. A mere overlooking pardon would not be worthy of him, nor would it help man. It would be the lack of mercy, the indifference, of a god who in truth is not God.

Question 10 speaks of the *curse* of God. This concept occurs again in questions 29, 39, and 52. In biblical usage the meaning of this word is at once simple and radical. When a person is called cursed in the Bible, that means quite simply that he is no longer inside but outside. As one who belongs to the covenant of God he is condemned to exist as one who does not belong to it, as one who is excluded. Curse means the rejection of the chosen, dismissal from the sight of God, banishment to the shadow and night and chaotic side of creation, exile to an existence without ground and possibility—all this for the creature who was destined to dwell in light! Curse does not mean the annihilation of man, release from being, but banishment to being in negation, in the sphere toward which God turned his back already at creation when he separated light and darkness. The Old Testament describes this existence as the shadow life of Sheol. The New Testament describes it as man's being in "hellish anxieties and torment" (q. 44). It is the existence which befalls those who are God's enemies, the existence of the human who through sin has become inhuman, who can continue to exist only in his lost human existence. That is man's misery. Questions 3-9 speak of the cause of this misery. Now in questions 10-11 we hear of the misery as such, of the situation which has become inevitable as a result of man's guilt. In this situation is made manifest the eternal downfall of man, the shadow of which falls back over his life from its end. That is what makes man fundamentally in need of comfort.

From what source do we know of this verdict of God? How do we know about this revelation of his terrible wrath, about this existence of man under his curse? Can we catch sight of it in the life of man, perhaps in our personal or in the general situation? Such insights change in a way quite similar to the way we have seen that opinions about man's goodness or wickedness change. There have been times when such concepts as curse, hellish anxiety, and torment were quite strange, and when they were dismissed as all too medieval. There have been other times—perhaps ours is such a time—when one understands very well what these concepts mean, when one experiences something of God's terrible wrath. But a really genuine recognition of God's wrath and curse, real knowledge of hellish anxiety and pain, would have to shake man so radically that it completely changed his whole being and life and thinking. It would have to evoke such terror that it really transferred man from his old condition to a new, quite different one. When there is no trace of that, we should be careful about thinking that we know anything of God's wrath and our guilt. We have not yet known what it means when we are shocked and horrified by the picture of human misery as we see it, and as Jaspers thinks he can recognize it in so-called "boundary situations." We know of such things today in middle Europe! Whole nations in these years have been led into such "boundary situations"! The Bible also knows of such situations for the individual and for nations. It speaks of famine and earthquake and war and mass death as divine judgments. But it also knows that these judgments of God come and go, that these things do not reveal the true and final shattering of man, the fundamental change in his condition. Let us ask ourselves: What does the suffering which has fallen upon humanity in these past years mean for our thinking and our total existence? Have not things gone as they did already with Samaria and Jerusalem? Judgments of God came. Things happened which thirty years ago we would have thought impossible. Six million Jews were murdered. Fire fell from heaven. Whole nations were led into exile. Horror and agony of every kind fell upon humanity. But all that has come and gone as a wind blows over the grass and flowers: they are bowed for a while, but when the wind stops, they raise themselves up again. Is there a single man who has really become fundamentally different because of the falling bombs? And if it should become yet a little worse than it was, things would hardly be any different. Could atom bombs change and renew man? The very thought is absurd!

The judgments of God obviously become effective in a quite different context. They do not have their genuine and truly shaking effect in themselves, nor in events as such, even when the agony is ever so great and the catastrophies ever so terrible. They are really effective only when in storm and tempest (or perhaps even more likely in a still, gentle sighing) the *Word of God* is heard. Falling houses and collapsing walls are not the Word of God. The Word of God is *Jesus Christ* or it is not the Word of God but one of the many words that come and go. But because it is Jesus Christ, it is also true that this Word of God speaks the verdict upon sinful man. This Word shows us the weight of the wrath of God, the hellish anxiety and pain into which man in himself has hopelessly fallen. To hear this Word of God is to be placed in a situation for which "boundary situation" is an all too mild description. It is the real situation of man before God in which he must confess himself to be enemy and rebel in relation to God.

We can test the genuineness of our knowledge of God's wrath and our guilt by asking whether it includes also this knowledge, whether it exposes our lostness and condemnation in such a way that we can no longer escape it by ourselves, in such a way that we can no longer survive it as we survive the catastrophes of our time, so that we cannot say in the words of a modern drama, "Once again we got by." Here one does not "get by." In this knowledge of the Word of God one is held fast. (Paul speaks of an imprisonment of the reason.) But the catechism speaks of the knowledge of our guilt and of divine judgment only when it speaks of Jesus Christ. In *him* this is revealed. For he himself is the one on whom God's wrath has been revealed. He is the man who has borne and suffered under this burden. Jesus Christ did not "get by." And if we Christians belong to this Christ, we also cannot get by, for we cannot get around him. He stands before us as the rejected one. "Upon him was the chastisement that made us whole" (Isa. 53). And because it lies on him, we are bound in him to take it seriously. It is only at this one place where God's wrath has burned as a consuming fire—Golgotha. There is where the judgment of God on man is revealed.

But because it is revealed in Jesus Christ, this verdict of God cannot be understood as a *last* word. What the wisdom of the existentialist philosophers can say as a last word about human existence, thank God, is just not the ultimate but is as provisional and finally as unreal as the wisdom of the ancient Stoics. Knowledge of man's misery in Jesus Christ does not lead us to resignation. It shows us rather the misery of man as a penultimate reality. It shows us his existence under God's wrath as that of a man who nevertheless is not lost. It speaks of the "deep hidden Yes" of the gospel in the midst of its "No." It is full of the comfort of the presence of the gracious God. He has borne what we have earned. That is the divine judgment which is revealed on Golgotha. *There*, where we see rejected and condemned man, man without rights, just there is man's right before God established again and honored. That is the real comfort, the last word in the burning of God's wrath. So must we understand man's misery, and so therefore must we read also the staggering questions 10 and 11 of our catechism. It is a comfort that it is Jesus Christ who reveals God's verdict on man.

It is noteworthy that the catechism speaks here only of the objective side of man's misery. Many subjective things might also be said about the misery of the man who must live without the Holy Spirit and who therefore cannot be willing and ready to serve God with his life and to praise him. The catechism breaks off its discussion with the question of the divine and human right. That seems enough to the authors, and it is enough. For everything further which might be said about human misery is included in the statement that this right is violated and destroyed. For this reason the part of the catechism dealing with man's misery can be so comfortingly brief. It must be there, and it must be taken with complete seriousness. But it would be good if sermons also were controlled by the discipline and restriction the catechism exercises at this point. Talk about human misery could easily become endless, but just this, thank God, is not endless. If the world has the impression that the church is a sighing and complaining thing, the reason to a large extent is the false proportions of our sermons. There is a dam which limits and holds back the floods of human misery. That must be seen also in the outline of sermons.

6 / *God's Righteousness*

(QUESTIONS 12-18)

The order destroyed by man is reestablished, the danger threatening him turned away, by the fact that in the one Jesus Christ God has taken up the cause both of his own right and of man's right, and in Christ guaranteed both the salvation of man and his own honor. The hope and the ground of all comfort is that this has happened in Jesus Christ.

Question 12. **Since, then, by the righteous judgment of God we have deserved temporal and eternal punishment, how may we escape this punishment, come again to grace, and be reconciled to God?** God wills that his righteousness be satisfied; therefore, payment in full must be made to his righteousness, either by ourselves or by another.

The second part of the catechism deals with "man's redemption." The place given to the three individual sections in the total structure of the catechism is statistically noteworthy. Nine questions deal with man's sin and guilt, 74 questions with his redemption, and 26 questions with his thankfulness.

Questions 12-18 contain a kind of foundation; questions 19-23, introductory statements about faith; questions 24-25, a short discussion of God as the sum of the object of faith; questions 26-58, the exposition of the creed; questions 59-64, concluding statements about faith; questions 65-85, a discussion of the sacraments.

In the edition of the Heidelberg Catechism edited by August Lang (*Heidelberger Katechismus*, 1907, p. lxxxix) one reads that the section composed of questions 12-18 is undoubtedly one of the weakest sections of the entire catechism because the whole manner of these questions is "artificial and purely theologizing" and allows us to miss the inwardness of the relationship between Christ and the believing community. This is without doubt a false judgment. Only apparently does the catechism develop the knowledge of man's redemption from an a priori deduction which postulates the reality of Jesus Christ from general presuppositions. That is, only apparently does it ask first, "If there is to be a redemption, in what must it consist and what must be the nature of the Redeemer?"; and then find the question accidentally answered concretely by Jesus Christ and his work. The catechism simply follows here the way of Anselm and of the Letter to the Hebrews: "Therefore he *had* to be made like his brethren in every respect" (2:17); "for we *had* to have such a high priest" (7:26). What *could* seem to be an a priori deduction in the questions and answers of the text of the catechism is rather, by virtue of the accompanying *proof texts,* an *analysis* of the fact of Christ to which the Old and New Testaments bear witness. This proof from Scripture is developed in the following way: With *question 12,* Romans 8:3 f. is cited: God sent his Son to fulfill the requirements of the law. With *question 13,* Matthew 6:12: "Forgive us our debts. . . ." With *question 14,* Hebrews 2:14 f.: The work of Jesus Christ as our brother is that "through death he might destroy him who has the power of death, that is, the devil, and deliver all those who through fear of death were subject to lifelong bondage."

With *question 15,* 1 Corinthians 15:21 is quoted: ". . . as by a man came death, by a man has come also the resurrection of the dead." Also Jeremiah 23:6, 33:16: "The LORD is our righteousness" is the name of Israel or Jerusalem. Also Isaiah 7:14: "Immanuel." And 2 Corinthians 5:21: "who knew no sin." And Hebrews 7:16: "Priest . . . by the power of an indestructible life."

On *question 16*, 1 Peter 3:18 is cited: "Christ also died for sins once for all, the righteous for the unrighteous. . . ." On *question 17*, Acts 20:28: ". . . the church of the Lord which he obtained with his own blood." And John 1:4: "In him was life. . . ."

Isaiah 53 is quoted in questions 15, 16, and 17 as the basic agreement in all three.

Precisely at this point the catechism intends to show by its arrangement and conception of the questions and answers that the fact of Christ, the ground of man's redemption, is not an accidental and arbitrary fact but a meaningful, necessary, logical happening (Logos!) in which the wisdom of the divine decree is revealed.

Question 18. **Who is this mediator who is at the same time true God and a true and perfectly righteous man?** Our Lord Jesus Christ, who is freely given to us for complete redemption and righteousness.

"Redemption and righteousness" is to be understood as "redemption *through* righteousness." We do not have to do here with two acts, but with the one act of the redemption which is given us in our Lord Jesus Christ in his fulfillment of God's assertion and restoration of his own and man's right. God is due recognition as the Lord; man is due life under this lordship. God's right and man's right are threatened by sin. God's act as Redeemer restores both. He defends his right and his honor, but he does it in just such a way that he also takes up man's destroyed right. Jesus Christ assumes responsibility for man before God. He "pays" for sin (qq. 12, 13, 16). He bears the burden of God's wrath (qq. 14, 17) and thereby removes the abnormal condition of man. He establishes God and man in their right again. Because that is the Christ event, it is the event of our redemption and thus the act of God's mercy (q. 11) by which his righteousness is "satisfied" (q. 12). Questions 13-17 are to be understood on this basis.

Question 13. **Can we make this payment ourselves?** By no means. On the contrary, we increase our debt each day.

Man cannot satisfy God's righteousness. He cannot restore the right of God and of man. In fact he himself is the ever new, ever recurring cause of the destruction of this right.

Question 14. **Can any mere creature make the payment for us?** No one. First of all, God does not want to punish any other creature for man's debt. Moreover, no mere creature can bear the burden of God's eternal wrath against sin and redeem others from it.

Another creature cannot "pay" because man is the one who committed the violation. He is questioned about his deed and he must answer for it. Moreover, no mere creature can reestablish the right of God and man.

Question 15. **Then, what kind of mediator and redeemer must we seek?** One who is a true and righteous man and yet more powerful than all creatures, that is, one who is at the same time true God.

Redemption as redemption through righteousness is only possible through one who is *true man,* one who is able to measure up to the responsibility of man before God, one who is capable of representing a new man (q. 16). But at the same time he must also be *true God,* one who is capable of actually achieving the restoration in its significance for all other men (q. 17).

Question 16. **Why must he be a true and righteous man?** Because God's righteousness requires that man who has sinned should make reparation for sin, but the man who is himself a sinner cannot pay for others.

Question 17. **Why must he at the same time be true God?** So that by the power of his divinity he might bear as a man the burden of God's wrath, and recover for us and restore to us righteousness and life.

Jesus Christ is the one who is able to do this (q. 18). He is our complete redemption through righteousness. He is the necessary, meaningful, logical ground of our redemption. He reveals the wisdom of God's decree. To know him, therefore, is to know clearly and surely, to think both ontically and noetically in a correct way in this matter of redemption. His existence cannot be deduced and postulated a priori; it can and must be understood after the fact. The church knows what it is doing when it knows and praises in him our "only comfort," for he is God's righteousness and therefore also his mercy in person.

He, Jesus Christ, has been given to us for redemption through righteousness. *In him* it is already *complete.* Its completion *in us* is the event of the *fulfillment* of this promise, the event of the final revelation of God's judgment, which has not yet happened (q. 52). "For we must all appear before the judgment seat of Christ" (2 Cor. 5:10). "For through the Spirit, by faith, we wait for the hope of righteousness" (Gal. 5:5). "But according to his promise we wait for new heavens and a new earth in which righteousness dwells" (2 Peter 3:13), and in which not only will he be our redemption through righteousness, but "we shall be like him" (1 John 3:2), and "appear with him in glory" (Col. 3:4). Meanwhile, we can only seek the "things that are above," our life "hid with Christ in God" (Col. 3:2 f.). In him—there is our redemption through righteousness. We *are saved*—but *in hope* (Rom. 8:24). Both things must be emphasized. But today we must throw our weight more strongly than the sixteenth century did on the fact that the completion of our redemption, *our* place in the restored order of God, is a matter of our hope, the event of the return of Jesus Christ in his revelation.

7 / The Revelation of God's Righteousness

(QUESTIONS 19-23)

The first fruit of the righteous act of God in Jesus Christ is the existence of those for whom as a living Word he has become the good news of redemption. It is the existence of those who believe in him, who in thankful recognition of the promise given in him and in trust in his truth have become his body, his people, and who therefore have been made the light of the world.

The interpretation of the creed, which forms the middle part of the catechism, is bracketed by sections which deal with *faith:* questions 19 ff. and questions 59 ff. These sections answer the following question: How does it happen in a preliminary way, here and now, before the final revelation of God's judgment, before the return of Christ, in our time, that the redemption through righteousness which has happened once for all in Jesus Christ is also real to us and recognizable as redemption? Redemption through righteousness has not only happened; because it has happened, it has also become manifest and effective. God's work was also God's Word. In acting, God also spoke. But God's Word is a creative Word which bears fruit. And its first fruit is that it finds *witnesses,* a witnessing people. The New Testament uses in this context the concepts *aparche* (first fruits) or *arrabon* (pledge, down payment). The existence of this people is a first thing which promises something greater. In this people who can understand their existence only in the Word of God, redemption through righteousness becomes provisionally and relatively but most effectively an event and recognizable as such.

Question 19. **Whence do you know this?** From the holy gospel, which God himself revealed in the beginning in the Garden of

Eden, afterward proclaimed through the holy patriarchs and prophets and foreshadowed through the sacrifices and other rites of the Old Covenant, and finally fulfilled through his own well-beloved Son.

The ground of redemption through righteousness is the covenant between God and man which was made already in and with creation. Redemption is therefore not an accidental event. It begins and takes shape in the history of the people of Israel. The one covenant achieves historical form in the making of a series of covenants. This covenant is fulfilled, however, in the existence of the one Jesus Christ ("fulfilled through his own well-beloved Son"). Redemption has a history. In its essence it was from the beginning what it will be visibly at its goal: the "holy gospel," the divine promise to *all* men. "I am the light of the *world*" (John 8:12). Thus through the mediation of these first witnesses we also know about redemption.

Question 20. **Will all men, then, be saved through Christ as they became lost through Adam?** No. Only those who, by true faith, are incorporated into him and accept all his benefits.

All men have not yet perceived that redemption has happened. The light does not yet simply and obviously shine over all, and all who have seen it have not yet grasped it. Revelation is a matter of election and selection, a matter of being called and of a decision. To the distinctiveness of Jesus Christ as the Head of a new humanity there corresponds the distinctiveness of a small group of people in the midst of the world, a branch grafted into Israel (Rom. 11:17, 19), so that in this people a new beginning of all humanity may become real. "Of his own will he brought us forth by the word of truth that we should be a kind of first fruits of his creatures" (James 1:18). The existence of the people of God is not an end in itself, not a final goal. Rather: ". . . as our King, thou art willing and able to give us all that is good since thou hast power over all things . . . that by this not we ourselves but thy holy name may be glorified forever" (q. 128). "You are the

light of the world" (Matt. 5:14)—that is the meaning of the unique existence of this people of God.

Question 21. **What is true faith?** It is not only a certain knowledge by which I accept as true all that God has revealed to us in his Word, but also a wholehearted trust which the Holy Spirit creates in me through the gospel, that, not only to others, but to me also God has given the forgiveness of sins, everlasting righteousness, and salvation, out of sheer grace solely for the sake of Christ's saving work.

The being and doing of the people of God are described here. They belong to the humanity whose misery is described in questions 3-11. It is only through faith that they are distinguished from other men (q. 6). But those who believe are those to whom it has been given to know the truth of God in Jesus Christ, to grasp the promise and to place their confidence in it. Faith is not only a knowledge; it is also this "wholehearted trust." We are not concerned here with a particular theory, but with the certainty that redemption through righteousness is *also for me,* that *also my* sins are forgiven. The decisive act of faith is recognition of the gift of God as an existential gift. Where this act of faith becomes an event in men, there come together the people of God, the people who may bear witness to the world of redemption through righteousness because, by virtue of the revealed and believed Word, they were "there" in the truest sense.

Question 22. **What, then, must a Christian believe?** All that is promised us in the gospel, a summary of which is taught us in the articles of the Apostles' Creed, our universally acknowledged confession of faith.

Question 23. **What are these articles?**
I believe in God the Father Almighty, Maker of heaven and earth; And in Jesus Christ, his only-begotten Son, our Lord: who was conceived by the Holy Spirit, born of the Virgin Mary; suffered under Pontius Pilate, was crucified, dead, and buried; he descended into hell; the third day he rose again from the dead; he

ascended into heaven and sits at the right hand of God the Father Almighty; from thence he shall come to judge the living and the dead.

I believe in the Holy Spirit; the Holy Catholic Church; the communion of saints; the forgiveness of sins; the resurrection of the body; and the life everlasting.

Here we are concerned with *doctrine.* The people of God who exist for the sake of their commission stand in need of a "certain *knowledge.*" Because we have to do here with the Word of God, with the Logos and his proclamation in human words, we need this knowledge as the basis of all our speaking. The creed, the "articles of our universally acknowledged confession of faith," contains the standard of knowledge (qq. 19, 21) which is common to these people wherever they are, without which no one belongs to them, without which they cannot fulfill their commission. In short, the creed contains what is necessary for a Christian to believe.

The preceding discussion of questions 19-23 deliberately goes beyond the literal meaning of the catechism in three respects:

1. Corresponding to the eschatological character of redemption through righteousness as it is set forth in paragraph 6, we have emphasized the *preliminary* character of revelation and faith. "For in this hope we were saved" (Rom. 8:24). "For now we see in a mirror dimly" (1 Cor. 13:12). And we have understood the people of God only as the *first* fruit (*aparche*) of the redemption which has happened.

2. We have not only spoken of the faith of the individual as the decision concerning his personal salvation, but of faith as the common equipping of the *people* of God. Thus we have understood faith not only in terms of the individual but also in terms of the church.

3. We have understood the faith of these people as the equipping of Christians for their task in the *world,* for their sending as bearers of the gospel, as light of the world—in contrast to the somewhat egoistic, narrow, and "stuffy" atmosphere which might otherwise be easily suggested by question 20.

8 / *The One True God*

(QUESTIONS 24-25)

God is exactly, completely, and exclusively what he has revealed himself to be in his Word: Father, Son, and Holy Spirit. That is, he is the Lord of the eternal kingdom for which the man may hope who is created, redeemed, and sanctified by him.

These two questions contain the Heidelberg Catechism's doctrine of God.

Question 24. **How are these articles divided?** Into three parts: The first concerns God *the Father* and our *creation;* the second, God *the Son* and our *redemption;* and the third, God *the Holy Spirit* and our *sanctification.*

Question 25. **Since there is only one Divine Being, why do you speak of three, Father, Son, and Holy Spirit?** Because God has thus revealed himself in his Word, that these three distinct Persons are the one, true, eternal God.

Scholastic theology, like the theology of the seventeenth and eighteenth centuries and also modern theology, followed a complicated course in the doctrine of God: (1) It constructed a supreme, infinite, omnipotent, etc., Being; (2) it had to show the identity of this God with the God of the Old and New Testaments (Exod. 3:14); (3) it tried to prove that he exists; (4) it wanted to prove the three-in-one character of this Being. The Heidelberg Catechism also knows of "one Divine Being," but it immediately defines this Being as the one "who has revealed himself in his Word" (qq. 25, 94, 95, 117), that is, as the one who has made himself clear and intelligible in the revelation of the redemption through righteousness which has happened in Jesus Christ. The catechism thus limits itself to the acts of God and derives from

them their Subject. God is the one who acts in a particular way
and in this acting proves his existence. This God is the three-in-
one God, the God whom the Apostles' Creed confesses in its three
articles: God the Father in his work of creation, God the Son in
his work of redemption, and God the Holy Spirit in his work of
sanctification.

The man redeemed in Jesus Christ hopes as such for the coming
of the eternal kingdom of freedom, the Lord of which is his *Redeemer,* God the Son. *This* is God.

The man redeemed in Jesus Christ sees the ground of his existence and of all existence generally in the kingdom for which he
hopes. He thus sees in the Lord of this kingdom his *Creator,* God
the *Father. This* is God.

The man redeemed in Jesus Christ finds himself already here
and now included in this kingdom, and so he knows its Lord as
the one who *sanctifies* him, the *Holy Spirit. This* is God.

God the Redeemer, God the Creator, God the Holy Spirit,
"these three distinct Persons" (q. 25), are—they are not just said
to be; they *are*—"the one, true, eternal God," just as surely as
the one kingdom has these three forms and as such is eternal. "As
Thou wast before all time, so remainest Thou in eternity." This
is the way God, whose Word I "accept as true" (q. 21), has revealed himself in his Word. And God is exactly and completely
and exclusively what he has revealed himself to be.

He is *exactly* that. All attributes of God are predicates of this
one three-in-one Lord of the kingdom, the Father, the Son, and
the Holy Spirit. There is thus no concept with which we could
designate the being of God which could have any meaning apart
from the fact that the eternal God is this three-in-one God who
reveals himself as such. He is the Subject, and all predicates are
determined by this Subject. We cannot describe him with previously conceived concepts. He himself who meets us in his
Word is the Light which illuminates and judges all concepts.

He is *completely* that. There is no hiddenness, no abyss, in
God's being which could be deeper than his being as the Three-
in-One. There is no truth in him which is not this truth. It is
God's innermost being which he reveals to us in Jesus Christ. God

the Father is the Father of Jesus Christ. And God the Holy Spirit is the Spirit of Jesus Christ. Therefore there can also be no question about God's existence which is not already answered by his self-revelation in his Word and work, no confession of faith which first and last can mean anything but him only.

He is *exclusively* that. Every conception and every presentation of a God who is not this three-in-one God, however beautiful and profound it may be, can only set up an idol, a false image of God. This is the basis from which we must understand the monotheistic impulse of the catechism which appears in questions 29, 30, 80, 94, 95, 102, 125. The authors have no speculative interest in oneness; the, are concerned about the singleness of the three-in-one God revealed in Jesus Christ.

9 / God, the World, and Man

(QUESTIONS 26-28)

Everything that is, is created, upheld, and ruled by the one true God. Therefore the world is the theater and instrument of his righteous action, a mirror and echo of his living Word. And man, with whom God in Jesus Christ has bound himself, may count on the fact that, whether he sees it or not, already now and here he is not in foreign territory but in the house of his eternal Father.

These three questions contain the *doctrine of creation*. We may venture the statement that this is the backbone of all Christian doctrine. It does not stand somehow apart from the truth of our redemption through righteousness. It is not a preliminary, first word which is to be heard and understood by itself to begin with; it stands in immediate connection with the knowledge of our redemption in Jesus Christ. The doctrine of creation points to the one true God who is also our Redeemer. But our redemption presupposes our existence as living beings, as men, in the midst of the cosmos. Everything said about us in God's Word applies to us as such beings in the cosmos. As such we are "in misery" (qq. 3-9), "in this troubled life" (q. 26), "in adversity" (q. 28) with all its contradictions (q. 27). And to such living beings applies also the other thing, that they need redemption, that as such they are the objects of God's love.

This is what the doctrine of God's creation, preservation, and government of the world says: In the event of our redemption through righteousness in Jesus Christ it is also revealed that the whole *being of the world* in which we exist, although it is not a divine being, *belongs to God*. It is put there, upheld, and directed by him, and therefore to us who are redeemed in Jesus Christ it is not obstructive but can only be beneficial. Man may therefore count on the fact that, whether he sees it or not, he is already, here and now, not in foreign territory but in the house of the eternal Father.

But this knowledge, that of the first article of faith, lives from the knowledge of Jesus Christ and therefore from the knowledge of the second article, and from the knowledge of the Holy Spirit and therefore from that of the third article. In the event of our redemption through righteousness in Jesus Christ, and thus in God's becoming known to us in Christ as he who honors his own right and our right, also this is revealed: it is the *Ground of all being*, the Creator with unlimited power, who so acts. The Ground of all being, the Creator of all things, is none other than the holy and merciful God who meets us in Jesus Christ and in him brings his righteousness to victory. Since our being and the being of the world is *his* creation, this is how we exist. We do not come to Jesus Christ and to God's Word from some other direction, from some sort of dark realm of being or history; we come always and first of all from *this* orientation. As Redeemer he comes into his own possession (John 1:11). Even when those who belong to him do not accept him, they *are* his. When we believe in him and obey him, we do nothing extraordinary; for when he lays his hand on us, we experience what is basically *natural*. Apart from God's grace there is only non-being. But standing in God's

grace we are helped in our whole being. Our redemption in Christ means our *genuine* and *total* redemption.

Questions 26-28 are theological gems in the catechism which deserve more careful attention.

Question 26. **What do you believe when you say: "I believe in God the Father Almighty, Maker of heaven and earth"?** That the eternal Father of our Lord Jesus Christ, who out of nothing created heaven and earth with all that is in them, who also upholds and governs them by his eternal counsel and providence, is for the sake of Christ his Son my God and my Father. I trust in him so completely that I have no doubt that he will provide me with all things necessary for body and soul. Moreover, whatever evil he sends upon me in this troubled life he will turn to my good, for he is able to do it, being Almighty God, and is determined to do it, being a faithful Father.

"What do you *believe?*" The question does not ask, what do you know or what do you feel? The question put here is thus not Schleiermacher's question about a view or a feeling of the universe. It is the question, "What does the Word of God say to you? What do you cling to when you cling completely and exclusively to this Word?" The explanation of the first article is not some kind of "outer court" theology or Christian world view; we are concerned here with the one Word of God, and therefore with the one entry and way of knowledge: I believe.

I believe "that the eternal Father of our Lord Jesus Christ . . . is for the sake of Christ his Son my God and my Father. . . ." *That* is what God's Word tells me. *That* is what I hold to with respect to my being in the cosmos and to the being of the cosmos as such. The whole truth lies in the subject of this sentence: God created and governs man. It is just the eternal Father of our Lord Jesus Christ who as such is the First, the Highest, the Lord over all being and thus also over my being. He is the one who out of nothing created, upholds, and governs heaven and earth and all that is in them. He is the one who assumes and bears responsibility for their being there (*Dasein*) and for the way in which they are there (*Sosein*). But that is to say that the meaning, ground, and origin of Jesus Christ is also the meaning, ground, and origin of *all* being. And because he *is* that, he is also *revealed* as such. This sequence is ontically and noetically irreversible: *before* all being distinct from God, God is the eternal Father of the eternal Son who became flesh in time. And only then—on the basis of this Father-being and Son-being of God and of the resulting decision made in man's favor, on the basis of the fact that God gave his only begotten Son for man, on the basis therefore of his eternal decrees—only then was the world created. That is the order of being. And corresponding to it, the knowledge of Jesus Christ the Son (and through the Son the knowledge of the eternal Father) comes *before* the knowledge of being. It is true both ontically and noetically that all things were made through him (John 1:3).

The predicate of the sentence contains the comforting assurance that the God who creates and governs all being, the eternal Father, is *"for the sake of Christ his Son"* also *"my God and my Father."* How can we utter this enormous possessive pronoun "my"? How can and may we—how dare *I*—say that he is "my God" and "my Father"? We can and may do it because he has given us Jesus Christ for complete redemption and righteousness (q. 18). God presents himself to me as Father of this Son; he sees me as his Son's brother and thus as his own child (qq. 33, 120). It follows from this that I may *have confidence* in the meaning, ground, and origin of all being (the being in which also I participate), because I know it in Jesus Christ the Son. I may have confidence in the fact and nature of my being as his creature. I may summon the courage to live. In this world I am not away from home but in the house of my Father who is not against me but for me. He who governs and maintains the world does not threaten me, but provides me with every necessity of body and soul as he sees fit. He turns to my good all evil, danger, menace, weakness, and imperfection of the creaturely existence which simply by virtue of its distinction from God is threatened existence. He turns away the infinitely greater danger which follows from the fact that man has become sinner and is in conflict with the Ground of all being. He reigns also over the disorder which is the consequence of the foolishness and wickedness of the human heart. He governs also the evil which, though it does not come from him, has the dangerous being of non-being. He turns no into yes. "We know that in everything God works for good with those who love him." That means permission to live in the world as in the house of the Father in which nothing can any longer be dangerous to his child but everything leads to the goal. God can do what he wills. He can do it in his omnipotence, and he will do it because his omnipotence is the faithfulness of the Father who "for the sake of Christ his Son" wills the best for us.

Question 27. **What do you understand by the providence of God?** The almighty and ever-present power of God whereby he still upholds, as it were by his own hand, heaven and earth together with all creatures, and rules in such a way that leaves and grass, rain and drought, fruitful and unfruitful years, food and drink, health and sickness, riches and poverty, and everything else, come to us not by chance but by his fatherly hand.

This powerful and willing divine care and turning-to-my-good of which question 26 speaks is God's providence, *providentia Dei.* Providence means not only to "foresee" but, according to the old translation, to "over-see." *Dominus providebit:* God will provide. Over and in all creatures in one way or another—quietly or actively, known or unknown, always according to the decision of his wisdom—there is the "almighty and ever-present power of God," the *same* power in all the differences and contradictions, light and dark sides, of creation. At this point all arbitrary optimism and pessimism err in their evaluation of creation because they believe that from a freely chosen standpoint they can judge how God's power orders both sides in the direction of his final goal, in the service of his coming kingdom, looking forward to the revelation of his majesty. Everything is very good, because everything is created and destined and therefore also suitable, whether we see it or not, for *his* service. God the Creator who is also Redeemer, the Father of Jesus Christ, makes no mistakes. God's power is God's "fatherly hand," "the Head of his church, through whom the Father governs all things" (q. 50). This "hand" of God is not just an image, an "anthropomorphism" as one usually says, by which we attribute to God our conceptions. It is rather so that all these conceptions have their original and genuine reality in him, and that everything we know is only an "image" of *his* reality.

Nothing is said here of the idea that God governs the world with his "left" hand. Rather, when the Bible speaks of the hand of God it always means his right hand. With it he governs *all things* (q. 50). Because of this government of his, the whole realm of being becomes the theater and instrument of his righteous action, the mirror and echo of his living Word, the parable of the kingdom of heaven. This has nothing to do with a mystique of created being, with Goethe's idea that everything perishable is a parable. It is rather so that all creation, also on its dark and evil side, is enlisted to this service. The "goodness" of *creation* is that it serves this purpose, that it may and can fulfill this function. And the goodness of the *Creator* is that this actually happens, that his creation does in fact become the theater and instrument, mirror and echo, of his acts and his living Word. "The heavens declare the glory of God, and the firmament proclaims his handiwork." The cosmos now *becomes* a parable. God speaks and God acts now; it is now his free grace if we and the whole creation may join in praising him. The movement of his "fatherly hand" is necessary in order for this to happen. It has nothing to do with natural theology which seeks the "footprints of God" in created being and sets up idols. But the creative word, "Behold it is all very good," is *not* disproved by sin. Sin is not that powerful. There is still the possibility that by the free grace of God creation may ever again become a parable. The providence of God is nothing other than God's free grace, and God's free grace in Christ is providence.

Question 28. **What advantage comes from acknowledging God's creation and providence?** We learn that we are to be patient in adversity, grateful in the midst of blessing, and to trust our faithful God and Father for the future, assured that no creature shall separate us from his love, since all creatures are so completely in his hand that without his will they cannot even move.

Questions 26-27 speak of the objective content of the doctrine of creation and providence. Corresponding to that, we may now speak of the "advantage" on our side. First, there is *patience* which can wait for the bestowing of God's free grace and endure "in adversity," which holds fast to the fact that God will act in his good time, which does not despair when it sees no parables of the kingdom of heaven. Then there is *thankfulness*. When the demonstrations of God's free grace happen and become visible, it rejoices not only at the redemption of man but also at his existence in the cosmos and at the existence of the cosmos as such. And it lives and acts in accordance with this joy—even today, in the year 1947! Finally there is *trust,* which through all contradictions holds to God himself, in everything praising him (his hand!) because nothing in all creation can separate us from him.

In all three of these concepts we are concerned with *faith* and thus not yet with sight. As redemption through righteousness in Jesus Christ has already happened and yet for us is still to happen in the future, so the continuity of providence is already present in God's government of the world but yet to be unveiled to us. Meanwhile it is right in patience and thankfulness and trust to continue faithfully with the Word that the Word may continue with us!

10 / *Jesus and His Brothers*

(QUESTIONS 29-34)

Corresponding to the sovereignty of the one true God over the world he created is the lordship of the one Jesus Christ over believing people who have been called by him, freed by him, and made responsible to him. He is their Lord because the right of God and of man established in him protects and binds them also.

We come to the series of questions and answers in the creed entitled "God the Son." It is instructive again at this point to notice the proportions: 3 questions are given to the first article, 24 to the second, and 7 to the third.

Questions 29-34 are an explanation of the first statement of the second article of the creed: "I believe in Jesus Christ, his only-begotten Son, our Lord." Questions 29-30 explain the name *Jesus;* questions 31-32, the title *Christ;* question 33, the mystery of Jesus Christ as *God's Son;* question 34, his status as *Lord.* As in other places, the Heidelberg Catechism is careful here also to connect statements about who God is with what he has done for us. Therefore the title of this section must read: "Jesus and His Brothers."

We have here a parallel to questions 26-28. There the subject is the sovereignty of God in the narrower sense, in the particular form of the lordship of Jesus Christ among his own. Now the sovereignty of God appears as the element which constitutes the church—the church which comes from One and in which only One can rule (qq. 29-30). Christians are those who are aware of Jesus Christ, thankfully owe him everything, and thus are joined to him as his members. But those who are called by him are (as *aparche,* first fruits) freed and protected by him and only him; and they are responsible and bound to him and only him (q. 32). So already in these first questions dealing with Christology it is clear that the doctrine of man's thankfulness necessarily follows, indeed is already contained in, the doctrine of man's redemption. The power of God's kindness to and claim upon man which shines in the church as the meaning and goal of God's will is already included in the name, title, mystery, and status of Jesus Christ. All this points to one thing, that in him has happened what had to happen: the right of God and the right of man were reestablished (qq. 12-18, 35-44, 45-49).

Question 31. **Why is he called Christ, that is, the anointed one?**

Because he is ordained by God the Father and anointed with the Holy Spirit to be *our chief Prophet* and *Teacher,* fully revealing to us the secret purpose and will of God concerning our redemption; to be *our only High Priest,* having redeemed us by the one sacrifice of his body and ever interceding for us with the Father; and to be *our eternal King,* governing us by his Word and Spirit, and defending and sustaining us in the redemption he has won for us.

This is a development of the recognition that Christ is of Israel, the King of the Jews, the Fulfiller of the Old Testament. He is the bearer of the charismatic offices prefigured in the Old Covenant: *Priest* by offering up his blood, *King* by his Spirit (q. 1!), *Prophet* in his self-revelation in the gospel (qq. 19-23). The eternal Word of the Father was a Jewish man who realized the election and calling of this people in his threefold office. The Redeemer through righteousness and our redemption can be had in no other way. Old and New Testaments, Jews and Christians, belong inextricably together.

Question 34. **Why do you call him our Lord?** Because, not with gold or silver but at the cost of his blood, he has redeemed us body and soul from sin and all the dominion of the devil, and has bought us for his very own.

As Redeemer he is our Lord and Owner. The claim on us of the majesty of Christ rises from the immeasurable kindness for which we have to thank him.

Question 33. **Why is he called God's only-begotten Son, since we also are God's children?** Because Christ alone is God's own eternal Son, whereas we are accepted for his sake as children of God by grace.

Where does Jesus Christ get this power to be Prophet, Priest, and King in one person, and therefore our Lord? He is not only a man like us, nor is he a middle being between God and man; he is God's only-begotten Son, "true and eternal God" (q. 35). Christ and only he is the *natural* Son of God, who by virtue of his sonship makes us to be children of God. He for whom it was not enough that he himself was God's Son (Phil. 2) became man that we might become what he is—God's child. He is that by nature, we by grace, placed through him in full and unreserved fellowship with God.

Questions 29 and 30 are to be understood on this basis.

Question 29. **Why is the Son of God called Jesus, which means Savior?** Because he saves us from our sins, and because salvation is to be sought or found in no other.

Question 30. **Do those who seek their salvation and well-being from saints, by their own efforts, or by other means really believe in the only Savior Jesus?** No. Rather, by such actions they deny Jesus, the only Savior and Redeemer, even though they boast of belonging to him. It therefore follows that either Jesus is not a perfect Savior, or those who receive this Savior with true faith must possess in him all that is necessary for their salvation.

Both questions make an exclusive statement: Since he *alone* is the eternal Son by nature and since he *alone* can redeem (qq. 12-18), since we do not belong to ourselves but to *him* (q. 34), therefore our redemption through righteousness is to be expected *only from him.*

But since he and only he is our Redeemer ("perfect Savior" or not Savior at all), the recognition of any other, or hope from any other source, would mean *denial* of Jesus Christ, "even though they boast of belonging to him." According to Catholic doctrine Christ is surrounded by a whole court of saints. That is "cursed idolatry" which for the sake of the uniqueness of the Redeemer we can only resolutely reject. But in so doing we must of course not overlook the fact that also in modern Protestantism, salvation is sought "by their own efforts, or by other means." The worship of the individual which is common here, and the absolutization of certain ideologies and theologies, encroach upon the uniqueness of the Redeemer no less than the Catholic veneration of saints. Legitimate theology can only point away from men to him, and his church is alive only when that happens. He is the *One* to his brothers or they are not his brothers.

Question 32. **But why are you called a Christian?** Because through faith I share in Christ and thus in his anointing, so that I may confess his name, offer myself a living sacrifice of gratitude to him, and fight against sin and the devil with a free and good conscience throughout this life and hereafter rule with him in eternity over all creatures.

This question is one of the most interesting of the whole catechism. Since Jesus Christ is a perfect Savior, and since we may know and believe in him as such, our life is *shaped* by him. The members follow their Head. The Christian is a man who lives with Christ, who shares in his anointing. His life necessarily corresponds to the life of Jesus Christ; it cannot possibly be left to arbitrariness but receives a quite definite ordering. The Christian *confesses* his name. He *offers* himself to him as a sacrifice of thanksgiving (q. 43). He *fights* against sin and the devil "with free conscience" in this life, and in eternity he will rule with Christ. Confession, sacrifice of thanksgiving, battle, victory with free conscience—these are the "works" of his church. In Lutheran theology one usually speaks at this point of the *unio mystica* (mystical union). We are not concerned here with an *unio mystica*, however, but with a *unio activa* (active union). Notice very especially the "free conscience"! If the Heidelberg Catechism had been properly heard at this point, even if only by its own confessors, who knows whether the "Enlightenment" together with the French Revolution and various other revolutions might not automatically have become unnecessary! We find nothing of "works righteousness" here, but rather an understanding of the existence of the Christian from that of his Lord. We can already see the outlines here of what will be spelled out later in the section of the catechism dealing with "Man's Gratitude."

11 / The Right of God in Jesus Christ

(QUESTIONS 35-44)

God's right consists in the majesty of his free grace exercised in Jesus Christ. For God exercises his right by giving himself in Jesus Christ (1) to take upon himself the curse, punishment, and destruction of sin, (2) to kill and bury the old sinful and wrong man, and (3) to bring again into being the new obedient man who is pleasing to him and who is the goal of all creation.

Questions 35-44 and 45-49 speak of the *work of Jesus Christ,* the redemption through righteousness (q. 18), reconciliation, *katallage,* exchange: God comes down to man; man rises up to God. Questions 35-44 speak of the condescension of God to the deepest depths of our being and existence—the *status exinanitionis,* the state of humiliation of the Son of God. It is the gospel of Good Friday, the *theologia crucis,* which is now developed.

Question 35. **What is the meaning of: "Conceived by the Holy Spirit, born of the Virgin Mary"?** That the eternal Son of God, who is and remains true and eternal God, took upon himself our true manhood from the flesh and blood of the Virgin Mary through the action of the Holy Spirit, so that he might also be the true seed of David, like his fellow men in all things, except for sin.

Question 36. **What benefit do you receive from the holy conception and birth of Christ?** That he is our Mediator, and that, in God's sight, he covers over with his innocence and perfect holiness the sinfulness in which I have been conceived.

Question 37. **What do you understand by the word "suffered"?** That throughout his life on earth, but especially at the end of it, he bore in body and soul the wrath of God against the sin of the whole human race, so that by his suffering, as the only expiatory sacrifice, he might redeem our body and soul from everlasting damnation, and might obtain for us God's grace, righteousness, and eternal life.

Question 38. **Why did he suffer "under Pontius Pilate" as his judge?** That he, being innocent, might be condemned by an earthly judge, and thereby set us free from the judgment of God which, in all its severity, ought to fall upon us.

Question 39. **Is there something more in his having been crucified than if he had died some other death?** Yes, for by this I am assured that he took upon himself the curse which lay upon me, because the death of the cross was cursed by God.

Question 40. **Why did Christ have to suffer "death"?** Because the righteousness and truth of God are such that nothing else could make reparation for our sins except the death of the Son of God.

Question 41. **Why was he "buried"?** To confirm the fact that he was really dead.

Question 42. **Since, then, Christ died for us, why must we also die?** Our death is not a reparation for our sins, but only a dying to sin and an entering into eternal life.

Redemption through righteousness means that redemption happens through a *judgment* in which the right of God as the presupposition of every human right is established again. The accusation of God stands. The sentence is executed. The wrath of God breaks out and burns and consumes sinful man (q. 37). The anathema, the "curse" (q. 39) happens. The "unspeakable anguish," the "hellish anxieties and torment" (q. 44), must be suffered. The debt must be paid with the death of the debtor. "God is not mocked, for whatever a man sows, that he will also reap."

When God's right is reestablished through judgment, it is revealed precisely in this judgment who God is. When he exercises his judgment and asserts himself as the Lord, it is not a matter of a triumph of God in the defeat of man but rather of his intervention for man. The right of God consists in his freedom not to destroy but to save the law-breaker. It consists in the majesty of his free grace. God does not will the death of the sinner, but that he repent and live. The depth of God and his righteousness is that he is totally strong and totally compassionate.

On this basis it becomes clear what sin is. The sin of the sinner is that it is the violation of the right of God—the right which is the right of his compassion. In exercising judgment and thus reacting in his grace to the rebellion of man, God *covers over* sin from his sight (q. 36). He does not want to see it. He puts it out of his sight. He banishes it to where it came from—into real "nothingness." This is how man is redeemed body and soul from everlasting damnation (q. 37), set free from the strict judgment of God (q. 38), so that even death can only serve the "dying to sin" and "entering into eternal life" (q. 42).

The fact that God's righteousness is his compassion becomes possible and real because *God himself descended* in order to make our affair his own. "The eternal Son of God, who is and remains true and eternal God, took upon himself our true manhood . . . that he might also be . . . like his fellow men in all things, except for sin" (q. 35). The power of this event, of this intervention of God for us, depends wholly upon the fact that no less than God himself was present in his Son. Because he is the eternal *true God* himself, he is able to bear what he does, "the wrath of God against the sin of the whole human race" (q. 37). He is able to pay the price (qq. 40, 42). A creature would not be capable of that. But as *true man* (q. 40) he "took upon himself the curse which lay upon me" (q. 39). He suffered for us, died for us. He made himself the brother of sinners, and as innocent man withstood temptation. "Sinlessness" is not simply an attribute of his human nature; it is his act of obedience. As one without sin he stood in our place in order to count as guilty before God. That is how Jesus answers the question of guilt: he takes it on himself—he the sinless and righteous one. Now, because he stands in this place, a *change* takes place. In the midst of humanity there happens something new, *the* new thing. The old condition is abolished.

God exercises righteousness in this self-giving by which he himself bears and suffers what we ought to bear and suffer. He does not exercise grace *instead of* justice, but he exercises grace *through* justice; and he exercises justice by exalting his grace. In the New Testament sense, grace is not *favor,* a friendly, patronizing attitude. It is *charis.* God is not too good to be our brother. He helps us. But our help is that Jesus Christ is our righteousness. God maintains justice, but it is *helpful* justice which does not take place for its own sake, but so that the world may live.

Question 43. **What further benefit do we receive from the sacrifice and death of Christ on the cross?** That by his power our old self is crucified, put to death, and buried with him, so that the evil passions of our mortal bodies may reign in us no more, but that we may offer ourselves to him as a sacrifice of thanksgiving.

Question 44. **Why is there added: "He descended into hell"?** That in my severest tribulations I may be assured that Christ my Lord has redeemed me from hellish anxieties and torment by the unspeakable anguish, pains, and terrors which he suffered in his soul both on the cross and before.

Here it is said, following Romans 6, that in the death of this one, all men (past, present, and future) have died, and as sinners and rebels against God have been eliminated and disposed of. Any sin and evil and foolishness which still happen have already been made obsolete at Golgotha: "the old *has* passed away." The alien power in the cosmos has been overthrown. Sin can now only be an anachronism.

And in the death of the guiltless one (qq. 35, 38) God has brought into being the thankful *new humanity:* "the new *has* come." In him creation has already reached its goal. He is the God-surrendered, thankful, new man (2 Cor. 5:17).

So on the one hand Jesus Christ creates a *past,* a world which was, the world of the old Adam, to which we cannot look back without freezing like Lot's wife. And on the other hand he creates a *future:* He not only shows us the way; he goes it himself and has already gone it for us. This is how he reestablishes the right of God and therefore the right of man. And as he stands in the middle between past and future it becomes true: "The kingdom of God has drawn near."

The subjective correspondence to question 43 will come in questions 88-90 in the doctrine of repentance.

12 / The Right of Man in Jesus Christ

(QUESTIONS 45-49)

The right of man consists in the wonder of the life given him through Jesus Christ. The right given to man is that in the resurrection of the one who is the Head of all, he was exalted to be the child of God, sanctified for God, made a participant already now in the coming revelation of God's kingdom, and assured his own victory over death.

Redemption through righteousness means an *act of judgment* in which the right of man also is restored as a consequence of the fact that the right of God is reestablished. This happens in the resurrection and ascension of Jesus Christ, in his *status exaltationis,* his state of exaltation. This is the gospel of Easter, the *theologia gloriae,* theology of glory. The revealed Word of God says both things: cross and resurrection, lowliness and majesty, of the true Son of God and Son of man.

In the death of Jesus Christ, God took man's place in order to suffer in his place the destruction of sinful man and, at the same time, to realize the existence of a new obedient man. The way is therefore open to restore the lost right of man, his right to live as the creature of God. The grace of God against which man sins triumphs in Jesus Christ. If the concept "human right" has a legitimate place anywhere, it is here in the Easter message. Apart from this it will have an empty ring, for man cannot call his own any right other than that won for him by God's righteousness which is compassion. It is true that light falls from this source on relative human rights and we may not silence talk about them. But such talk will be effective only when it is based on the life given to sinful men in the resurrection of Jesus Christ. Everything depends on the church's coming forward not with some kind of theory of self-salvation but with the Easter message. If the word about the right of man is not spoken with the full power of this message, it will not be spoken at all; it will resound only with the empty phrases of the newspapers and political parties which cannot even show man his right, much less create it.

We are concerned with the life of man through and before God, the life which triumphs because it is given him anew by divine action. The glory of human life becomes an event in the *resurrection of Jesus Christ*. He has not only suffered death for us, he has overcome it. As he stands for us in his humiliation at the end of the old man and his time, so he stands for us in his exaltation at the beginning of the new man and his time.

The decisive questions in this context are questions 45 and 49.

Question 45. **What benefit do we receive from "the resurrection" of Christ?** First, by his resurrection he has overcome death that he might make us share in the righteousness which he has obtained for us through his death. Second, we too are now raised by his power to a new life. Third, the resurrection of Christ is a sure pledge to us of our blessed resurrection.

Question 49. **What benefit do we receive from Christ's ascension into heaven?** First, that he is our Advocate in the presence of his Father in heaven. Second, that we have our flesh in heaven as a sure pledge that he, as the Head, will also take us, his members, up to himself. Third, that he sends us his Spirit as a counterpledge by whose power we seek what is above, where Christ is, sitting at the right hand of God, and not things that are on earth.

He is in heaven *for us.* He wills to make us participants in the righteousness won for us by his death. In reestablishing God's right and thus the triumph of God's grace by his death, he has also reestablished our right. In this way he is "our Advocate in the presence of his Father in heaven." In exalting the life of man in his resurrection Jesus revealed a human life which we cannot realize by ourselves and which is inaccessible to us even in his form—a life hidden "in heaven." He no longer lives among us as one whom we can see and hear and touch, but as one whom we can know only in the message of his resurrection. But just as such he is *our Advocate* with the Father. Everything which may still accuse us is opposed *there.*

Because Christ became our brother and as such rose from the dead, in him we also have already risen. In him our flesh is in heaven. Question 49 says therefore that "we have *our flesh* in heaven as a sure *pledge.*" He is the pledge of our own resurrection. We are his members; he is the Head who already exists in living exaltation. Will the Head abandon his members and not draw them after him? He is risen *for us!*

Finally he is in heaven for us in that he *"sends us his Spirit as a counterpledge* by whose power we seek what is above." The corresponding statement in question 45 is that "we too are now raised by his power to a new life." Since we belong to him, are already risen in him, and have in him the forerunner of our own resurrection, it cannot be otherwise than that we belong to him. He calls us. This call of the Risen One, the living Word of God which has been spoken once and for all, is what the New Testament calls the *Holy Spirit.* The Holy Spirit is not a spiritual current but simply the Word of God which comes to us and which we receive. But from whom could this Word come to us except from him who overcame death and exists not in the historical past but as our Advocate, our "pledge," in heaven before the Father and gives us the "counterpledge" of his Spirit? That is the power by which we seek what is above. Our seeking answers his seeking. And this is how we seek and find also our own life, our human right in power and glory. This is how we are already now awakened to a new life.

Question 46. **How do you understand the words: "He ascended into heaven"?** That Christ was taken up from the earth into heaven before the eyes of his disciples and remains there on our behalf until he comes again to judge the living and the dead.

It is as the Christ who "ascended into heaven" that he exists "on our behalf" as the Head of his members. If we are to understand correctly here, we must emphasize this: *He* is for us. *He*— this Subject distinguished from all the rest of humanity. He is just as different from us in his resurrection as in his death. Just as we must speak of his *objective* victory over death, so must we speak of his *objective* life in exaltation. This is a *historical decision* made *about* us and thus by no means first of all one which is made *in* us. We must in any case understand *objectively* (and this is the limit of a legitimate interpretation) the statement in question 46 that Jesus Christ was taken up from earth into heaven before the eyes of his disciples. This must not be reinterpreted to mean an inner elevation which men experience in fellowship with Christ. It is true that men do experience such. But first of all, decisively, and undergirding every elevation we share, we have to do here with the one Jesus Christ himself in his difference and distance from all other men. The conquest of death and the exaltation of life was an event in Jesus Christ the Head. His exaltation is history just as his humiliation is history. For this reason we must simply say No to Bultmann's "demythologization" of the New Testament. The "resurrection of Jesus Christ" means the resurrection of this one person distinguished from all others, and thus an event in time and space just like the event of Golgotha. If it does not mean that, this event is reduced to a new determination of human existence, to the awakening of faith in the first disciples. Then there is no Christ *for* us and *over* us to substantiate the existence of Christ *in* us. Then the Easter message as such is subverted and nullified. What is right about the attempt to "demythologize" the New Testament can only be the clarification of the obvious fact that from a literary-historical point of view the Easter message does in fact not have the character of *Historie* [i.e., history which is subject to the investigation and confirmation or refutation of the historical sciences]. What the Easter message reports does not occur in *Historie*. The historian will speak here of saga and legend. If Bultmann wanted only to say that we are concerned here with history (not myth!) in the form of saga and legend, there could be no objection to him. Why should we engage in hair-splitting arguments? But it is not possible to deny the really historical character of the account because it has this form. Why should not saga and legend be a quite appropriate tradition in cases in which the form of *Historie* has its natural limitations? The Bible contains innumerable sagas and legends. But it would be false to conclude from this fact that they are not the expression of real happenings. In no case does the Bible intend to present timeless truths or myths. And so also in this case, it intends to be genuine history (*Geschichte*), but history in a form inaccessible to *Historie*. The legitimate sequence here is Easter event—Easter message (saga!)—Easter faith (the contrary experience to the experience of the cross). Whoever begins with the Easter *faith* in order to make *it* the content of the Easter message and finally indulgently to let the Easter *event* fall away—his talk on this subject is boring and certainly not legitimate.

He is risen. *He* lives the fulfilled life of glory. In him that is revealed. This means that for us all this holds good only with reference to him. From our point of view, Christ the Risen One is our future goal, our promise. We wait for him until he comes (q. 49). He is our "pledge" (qq. 45, 49). We have to seek what is *above* (q. 49). All these statements refer to a "not yet." We *are* exalted to be God's children; we *are* participants in the coming kingdom; as those who live with death before us we *are* assured of our victory over death. Nothing is to be relativized or minimized here. Everything *is* completed. But it does not yet appear what we shall be. A cover still lies over us which will one day be taken away. In this sense it is not Christ's resurrection, but our resurrection and exalted life, which is the object of our expectation.

Questions 47 and 48 may be called a "theological disaster."

Question 47. **Then, is not Christ with us unto the end of the world, as he has promised us?** Christ is true man and true God. As a man he is no longer on earth, but in his divinity, majesty, grace, and Spirit, he is never absent from us.

Question 48. **But are not the two natures in Christ separated from each other in this way, if the humanity is not wherever the divinity is?** Not at all; for since divinity is incomprehensible and everywhere present, it must follow that the divinity is indeed beyond the bounds of the humanity which it has assumed, and is nonetheless ever in that humanity as well, and remains personally united to it.

On question 47: In the light of Matthew 28:20 ("Lo, I am with you always, to the close of the age.") only an unqualified yes would be the appropriate answer to this question. If it is true that Jesus Christ is true God and true man, then he is that under all circumstances. But here in question 47 an unfortunate distinction is made between his divine and his human nature. It lacks the simplicity of biblical thought and speech. What does "he is never absent from us" mean if it applies only to his deity, only to the Logos? Is there a presence of Christ "in grace and Spirit" in which his humanity is not also present?

On question 48: That the deity is "outside," *extra,* the humanity of Jesus Christ is correct as a description of the free grace of the incarnation. But *post Christum,* looking back to the incarnation from where we stand, this statement can only be one of unbelief. If we believe in Jesus Christ, we believe in this one person who is true man and at the same time true God.

With this criticism of questions 47 and 48, however, we do not mean to affirm the Lutheran position against which they are directed. Behind the Christological controversy stands the tragic controversy over the Lord's Supper in which, it seems to me, false theses were countered with false antitheses. It is the debate concerning the elements, "body and blood," *significat* and *est*. But in the New Testament the *est* without any doubt at all refers not to the elements but to the *action*. And whereas "body and blood" was understood in the debate to mean corporeality, the New Testament means by *soma kai haima* simply "man." One should thus by no means have spoken abstractly of corporeality as Luther did, so that Zwingli could only give a false answer to a falsely put question, and oppose corporeality with a pure spirituality which is just as foreign to the sense of the New Testament. The outcome was the Lutheran doctrine of the omnipresence or ubiquity of Christ which the Reformed theologians opposed with the assertion that it is not a matter of Christ's omnipresence but of his existence in heaven. This is the background of the formulations in questions 47 and 48. The controversy continued with the debate concerning the *Logos intra* or *intra et extra naturam humanam* [the Logos within or within and without the human nature]. Can we still continue this controversy today? Was not the whole thing abortive? We can learn from these two questions in the catechism how dangerous it is when one partner in a theological conversation lets himself be misled by a false thesis to make a false counterthesis. The Reformed theologians in the sixteenth century should not have let themselves be so misled by Luther that they began on their side to speculate and spiritualize. On no account can we unquestioningly take up again today the "confessional" differences which arose in this way, much less attribute to them a church-splitting significance.

13 / The Kingdom of Jesus Christ

(QUESTIONS 50-52)

The meaning and power of God's omnipotent reign in his creation is the rule of grace and life in Jesus Christ. His reign is exercised inwardly and directly through the special gifts of the Spirit in his church, but also outwardly and indirectly in his determination of the general and particular course of history. Jesus Christ is the hidden King of this whole kingdom. At the end of time he will be revealed as the Judge of all men.

Question 50. **Why is there added: "And sits at the right hand of God"?** Because Christ ascended into heaven so that he might manifest himself there as the Head of his Church, through whom the Father governs all things.

He who is true God and true man, he who has reestablished both the right of God and the right of man, he who is the humiliated and exalted one, he who is the Head of his church—he sits at the right hand of God. He who was and is and shall be is the subject of *all* divine action. Our time is the time of his present and his future, his lordship. It stands under the sign of the *change* which happened in his death and resurrection, in expectancy of his perfect future revelation. It is the *end-time*, the time hurrying from this hither to this thither.

In paragraph 10 on questions 29-34 we said that the lordship of the one Jesus over the people who believe in him *corresponds* to the sovereignty of the one true God. Why is it that we can speak of a correspondence here? Because the reigning will of God in Jesus Christ (thus in the work of his righteousness which is grace, and in the work of the life which is recognizable to the Christian church) is at the same time the secret, the meaning, and the power of the divine ruling and governing in creation in general. The "hand" which governs all things (qq. 27-28) is not some kind of dark power which manages and rules us however it likes; it is the hand of him who is revealed to us in Jesus Christ. The result of the incarnation, crucifixion, and resurrection of Jesus Christ is quite simply this: "All authority in heaven and on earth has been given to me" (Matt. 28:18). Sitting at the right hand of the Father, Christ is the Head of the Christian church. But this does not mean that he has one "province" in the world to lead, and that besides him there are other kings and leaders!

He is rather "the Head of his Church, through whom the Father governs *all* things" (q. 50). It is obviously one thing that Jesus Christ is the Head of his church and something quite different that the Father governs all things through him. He is the Lord of his church in a different way from that in which he is Lord of the whole world. This difference is not what is important, however, but the fact that both here and there his lordship is completely real and completely effective. His kingdom has no end. It is not limited by the walls of the church to the circle of Christians. The Lord of the church is also the Lord of the cosmos (Col. 1 and Eph. 1). He proves himself to be the "Head of his Church" (q. 50); that is, by virtue of his resurrection he is active and revealed as the first fruit of the new creation, the living Word of God who awakens, calls, and joins to himself the church to follow and serve him. And as such he is the ruler also of all other spheres of the world. The church stands *alongside* the world, but the Lord of the church stands *over* the world. Those who belong to him know the Father has given over *everything* to him.

Question 51. **What benefit do we receive from this glory of Christ, our Head?** First, that through his Holy Spirit he pours out heavenly gifts upon us, his members. Second, that by his power he defends and supports us against all our enemies.

The lordship of Christ as the Head of his Christian church is exercised *internally* and *directly* through the gifts of the Holy Spirit: faith, love, and hope. Wherever the church is founded, led, and built up, wherever on earth there is the life described in the apostolic letters (Rom. 12 and 14)—there we are confronted with the presence and reign of Jesus Christ. There his sitting on the right hand of the Father becomes effective. His power and rule are identical with the Word of God in the church. This is no "religious reality" but a fact, the fact that "by his power he defends and supports us against all our enemies."

But Christ also exercises his lordship and power *externally* and *indirectly*. Although in a different way, the course of history outside the church is just as much under his control as the course of the church itself. There is no such thing as a world history simply left to its own laws. There is no separation between general providence and the guidance of the church. In great and in small "histories" we have to do with the *time of grace:* by grace he protects his church against all enemies and preserves it for the sake of its task. The church is threatened but it does not go under: *perpetua mansura est* [its endurance is forever]. The church is God's affair; but the "works of the devil" (q. 123) oppose it. In question 51, therefore, "our enemies" does not mean first of all our personal enemies but the devil, the world, and our own sin (q. 127). The fact that in this time between Christ's resurrection and second coming there is a church history means that Christ has not abandoned the world. In this sense we can say that the church is the meaning and the secret of world history; world history takes place for the sake of church history. Here is the seat of real power against which all other powers are only "impotencies."

Question 52. **What comfort does the return of Christ "to judge the living and the dead" give you?** That in all affliction and persecution I may await with head held high the very Judge from heaven who has already submitted himself to the judgment of God for me and has removed all the curse from me; that he will cast all his enemies and mine into everlasting condemnation, but he shall take me, together with all his elect, to himself into heavenly joy and glory.

Here we look toward the future. The one who has come is also the one who will come. The judgment of God which is hidden in the course of life and the world, in which we may believe as the secret not only of the church but of the cosmos, will be *revealed*. This future *comforts* the church in all affliction and persecution because it *knows* the Judge. It knows that the judgment has already been executed—executed in such a way that this Judge "has already submitted himself to the judgment of God for me." The Judge is one who was judged for us. Through him we have been acquitted and from him we can now look forward to joy and glory. For only his enemies are condemned. Who are these enemies? Those mentioned in questions 123 and 127? We could understand it this way. But here in question 52 do we not see something of the medieval pictures of judgment day in which the "damned" are all too graphically depicted? The old theologians used to end their work with the doctrines of eternal blessedness and eternal damnation, and in this context to ask how the blessed feel when they think of the damned. The answer was that the thought does not trouble them; on the contrary, when they look at the damned they rejoice that God's honor is so great. It would be better to restrain ourselves here and not sing with Dante the song of paradise, much less the more famous song of hell. If we want to understand condemnation correctly, we must hold fast to the fact that all men (we too!) are his enemies—but that we all go to meet the Judge who gave himself for us. It is true that he is the *Judge;* there can be no doctrine of universal salvation. Nevertheless, he is the Judge whom we Christians may *know.* Would it not be better in the time of grace in which we still live to proclaim to men this good news, to tell them who our Judge is, rather than to reflect on whether there is an eternal damnation? We Christians are called to confess and bear witness that Christ died for all men. He is *the* Lord, beside whom there is no other. We may *believe* that—*for* his enemies also. We certainly should not weaken the seriousness of condemnation, but we should hold fast to the fact that Christ *suffered also for them.* Then the contrast between the elect (us) and the damned (them) can continue to concern us only humorously. For the elect who awaits his Judge with head held high there can be no alternative but to proclaim this Judge to those who do not yet know him and thus to remain in solidarity with all men. But this means that all pictures of judgment day are wrong. They are profoundly *unchristian* pictures.

The expression "sitting at the right hand of God," properly understood, clearly sets forth two fundamental principles of the Christian ethic:

1. Whoever understands that phrase correctly must also understand this: what is Christian takes unqualified *precedence* over everything else. Man is of course never only a Christian. He has

also his body, his eyes, his ears, his nose. He is a whole little cosmos. But everything else that he is, is subordinated to this one thing, that he is first of all a Christian. This sequence is not reversible. So, for instance, one can never be a politician and then also in the second place a Christian. Christianity cannot be coordinated. It takes absolute precedence—because Christ sits at the right hand of the Father.

2. But from a correct understanding of this "sitting at the right hand of God" there also follows the absolute necessity of *the relatedness of the Christian to the world,* the relatedness of the Christian to everything human. It is not so that as a Christian one may or may not be interested in what is human, perhaps have open eyes for what is beautiful and great and pleasant in the world and perhaps not. Relatedness of the Christian to the world is not optional. He cannot set himself against the world with the somewhat shabby mistrust in which as a Christian he thinks he knows everything better, or perhaps even with hostility. This is impossible because through his church and as its Head, Christ rules over *all.* We would be guilty of breaking up the lordship of Christ if we did not live in the world with open eyes and open hearts and did not will in all seriousness to be Greeks to the Greeks. After all, Christians are also creatures, and therefore they cannot evade the problems of the realm of creation. This realm also is subject to Christ, and we are at home in it also.

14 / God Is Spirit

(QUESTIONS 53-58)

In his being Holy Spirit, God is equally eternal, omnipotent, and merciful as in his being Father and Creator, and Son and Redeemer. God acts not only *over* and *on* but also creating life *in* the men who in faith belong to Jesus Christ, who through him are gathered into the church and made participants in its gifts and tasks. As sinners, by the power of his death, they may already here and now live without fear; by the power of his resurrection, they may here and now be joyful; therefore in this temporal life they may anticipate eternal life.

In the third article, *"I believe"* means to look back to the first and second articles and to say: I believe that *I* may exist, that God the Father-Creator and God the Son-Redeemer is also *my* Creator and Redeemer, so that I, too, am his creature and his redeemed one. As creature I may be a member of the church. I may defy my sin and my death. In the face of the frailty of my creatureliness, I may *expect my perfection:* I believe in an everlasting life (q. 58).

This "I believe" is the content of the third article. I believe—in my faith? No. I believe in God the Father and God the Son, and as I believe in him I believe also in the one true God who is also *Holy Spirit,* "equally eternal" with the Father and Son, the *Spiritus vivificans qui cum patre et filio simul adoratur et glorificatur* [the life-giving Spirit who with the Father and the Son together is worshiped and glorified].

When we understand the third article as the third form of faith in the one God, we become aware of the fact that here the answer is anticipated to a whole series of questions. The legitimacy of a whole series of peculiar Christian movements can be understood. A stream of open or secret mysticism has flowed through the whole history of Christianity: God and the soul, the soul and God. We think of everything called "pietism," whether of a more mystical or a more moralistic character. A correctly understood "I believe in the Holy Spirit" means freedom from what is desired here—or the acceptance of what is legitimate in it. To understand "I believe in the Holy Spirit" is to understand pietism also. The concerns of so-called neo-protestantism (or liberalism), classically represented by Schleiermacher, also lie on the same line of development as pietism. If we understand the third article, we may perhaps recognize even Schleiermacher in it. We may perhaps no longer need to think with wrathful indignation of him and the theologians of the 19th century with their "God in us" and everything connected with it. We may know the real conquest of liberalism; that is, we will not be in danger of crawling into this doll's house, yet we will recognize the genuine questions which lie hidden here. If our young theologians would see and recognize the confession of faith in its completeness, they could perhaps even become a little "liberal" again! Then they would not fall either into the pietistic or the liberal trap, nor would they have to become "orthodox." They could understand the faith with a certain naturalness and simplicity: "Everything is yours, but you belong to Christ." In other words, when we come to the third article, we are no less at the center of things than in the first and second articles. The God who as Father is my Creator, who as Son is my Redeemer, is the God who also creates life *in me*.

I believe in God the Holy Spirit.

Question 53. **What do you believe concerning "the Holy Spirit"?** First, that, with the Father and the Son, he is equally eternal God; second, that God's Spirit is also given to me, preparing me through a true faith to share in Christ and all his benefits, that he comforts me and will abide with me forever.

This is the inestimable central declaration of the third article: God does not will only to be over me; he is *in me*. *Deus in nobis!* Despite all neo-protestantism *and* all its opponents! What does it mean that he "is also given to me, preparing me through a true faith to share in Christ and all his benefits"? This *Deus in nobis*, this fact that the Holy Spirit is given to me, cannot for one instant be understood statically. Christ is given to me as the ground of my faith. Grounded in God, even our little bit of faith is true faith, that is, participation in Christ and all his benefits. In faith we reach out for what God gives us. I believe that I already participate subjectively (q. 1) in the comfort objectively created in Jesus Christ, and that this is not a passing but a final event. It is not possible in faith for faith to cease. If faith is taken away from me, I have thrown it away.

Questions 54 and 55 belong together.

Question 54. **What do you believe concerning "the Holy Catholic Church"?** I believe that, from the beginning to the end of the world, and from among the whole human race, the Son of God, by his Spirit and his Word, gathers, protects, and preserves for himself, in the unity of the true faith, a congregation chosen for eternal life. Moreover, I believe that I am and forever will remain a living member of it eternally.

Question 55. **What do you understand by "the communion of saints"?** First, that believers one and all, as partakers of the Lord Christ, and all his treasures and gifts, shall share in one fellowship. Second, that each one ought to know that he is obliged to use his gifts freely and with joy for the benefit and welfare of other members.

These questions deal with the church, the communion of saints. In believing in God the Holy Spirit, I do not believe only that *I* may believe. There is no private Christianity. In believing in the Holy Spirit, I believe in God's action for the benefit of *all* creation, to which in my faith I belong. Not I and my faith but the completion of his work is the goal of God's ways. God has lighted a light on earth. I believe that there is a *church* on earth, a community founded by the Son of God. It is not man who is primarily at work in this community (although there is of course praise of God, prayer, proclamation); everything happens here by the initiative of Jesus Christ. Wherever the church is, there he is active. There God himself "gathers, protects, and preserves." The founding and preserving of the church is his work. Where he is not, there is nothing. All heretical and all dead ecclesiasticism is the result of no longer grasping Christ as the *one* Foundation.

"Moreover, I believe that I am and forever will remain a living member of it eternally." To be a Christian means to be a living member of the church. And in this context we must say with complete seriousness, *extra ecclesiam nulla salus* [outside the church, no salvation]. We may say that it is a beautiful piece of theological thinking when the Heidelberg Catechism mentions the existence of the individual Christian only after it speaks of the existence of the church. But on the other hand, every individual is included just in this way.

Question 55 shows a second view of what the church means in the Apostles' Creed. In believing in the Holy Spirit, I believe in the *communion of saints*. In Latin [*communio sanctorum*] the problem arises here whether we are to think of the *sancti* [the communion of "holy people"] or the *sancta* [the communion of "holy things"]. We may assume that the Heidelberg Catechism intends both possibilities. The first sentence seems to point to *sancta*, the second to *sancti*. Every individual Christian is given full participation in the *gift* which is Christ himself. And on the other hand *each one* is called to give himself totally to serve the "benefit and welfare of other members" and just in this way to serve the benefit and welfare of all men.

Question 56. **What do you believe concerning "the forgiveness of sins"?** That, for the sake of Christ's reconciling work, God will no more remember my sins nor the sinfulness with which I have to struggle all my life long; but that he graciously imparts to me the righteousness of Christ so that I may never come into condemnation.

Question 56 says that to believe in the Holy Spirit is to hold to what has happened for me in the death of Jesus Christ because of the humiliation of the Son of God. It is to believe that my sins are forgiven, that "for the sake of Christ's reconciling work, God will no more remember my sins . . . so that I may never come into condemnation." The absoluteness of this "never" excludes every anxious look back into the past and every anxious look forward into the future. Anyone who would nevertheless still qualify this "never" would in reality set himself in rebellion against the lordship of Jesus Christ, who has decided the fact that *God* accomplishes his own and man's right. This right is now in effect. The whole of ethics rests on this article of the forgiveness of sin. It is the ground of the command given man. This "never" is no soft pillow; it proclaims the lordship of Jesus Christ which must necessarily give rise to *thankfulness* on man's side. Whoever wants to distinguish between (not to mention separate) faith and works has not understood the decisive point here. To believe means to be placed under the lordship of Christ and therefore also in the order of obedience. Everything done in this order depends of course on whether one believes in God and his Holy Spirit and not in an abstract forgiveness of sin.

Question 57. **What comfort does "the resurrection of the body" give you?** That after this life my soul shall be immediately taken up to Christ, its Head, and that this flesh of mine, raised by the power of Christ, shall be reunited with my soul, and be conformed to the glorious body of Christ.

Question 57 is related to question 56 as the *theologia gloriae* to the *theologia crucis*. In believing in the Holy Spirit I may believe that, because of the victory won by Jesus Christ, I may depend on my *conquest of death*. I shall die one day. But my end will only be the sign of a new beginning. Even if I die, I shall live.

In the light of the present understanding of biblical anthropology and eschatology, we would perhaps express differently what the catechism says here about soul and body. But the important thing is that it also speaks of the *whole* man, soul and body, who moves through death to a resurrection in which he will be conformed to the glorious body of Christ. The destroyed *right of man* is reestablished. And his right is that death does not mean a final catastrophe, but that he may live eternally with Christ. He is comforted because he goes to meet this future. In his resurrection I am promised—every one of us is promised— life with him. We may begin and live every new day with this hope. The Christian hope is unqualified. It is not the hope for a "higher life" or the dreadful idea that after death we must begin all over again and go back to school (a heavenly school or a school for angels, perhaps!). No, thank God! That is not what the New Testament says. Our hope for the future has to do with *this life* of ours. This life is not left behind or given up. It was and is and also will be *lived* before *him*. Man is man in his whole

life span, from baby to old man, and this man is the object of
the resurrection. All of him is flesh and by nature ought to perish.
That is what we truly deserve. But that is not what happens. Now
this whole life in its temporality is allowed rather to be "conformed" to the glorious life of Christ. That which is nothing
may, for the sake of Jesus Christ, now be something. God will
say yes to us, and no longer is there any bargaining involved in
this yes. The resurrection has nothing to do with education and
pedagogics, thank God. And lo, "it was very good."

Question 58. **What comfort does the article concerning "the life
everlasting" give you?** That, since I now feel in my heart the beginning of eternal joy, I shall possess, after this life, perfect blessedness, which no eye has seen, nor ear heard, nor the heart of
man conceived, and thereby praise God forever.

The everlasting life points to the *goal* of the resurrection. Man
is promised "perfect blessedness." But the "beginning" of eternal
joy is already given him here, because in the Holy Spirit he is
bound to Jesus Christ and may live united with him.

15 / God's Righteousness and Man's Faith

(QUESTIONS 59-64)

Faith is the confidence in which a member of the Christian community believes that in the death and resurrection of Jesus Christ,
God's righteous action has achieved its goal for all men and thus
also for him. The believer holds this in thankful obedience, but
without any dependence upon his own worthiness or accomplishment. Just for this reason it is a total and powerful comfort. Be-

cause faith has this content and because only faith corresponds to this content, faith and faith alone is man's way to justification.

Question 59. **But how does it help you now that you believe all this?** That I am righteous in Christ before God, and an heir of eternal life.

The content of the *second* article is God's righteous and saving action in Jesus Christ. The *first* article tells us that this happens by the power of him who is Creator and Lord of everything that is. The *third* article tells us that this Lord also gives us freedom to respond to God's action with faith. Questions 59-64 could be understood as a commentary on question 53: In believing in the Holy Spirit, we believe in him who gives us faith. I believe, *credo:* that means that I have a share in the results of God's action (cf. qq. 20, 32, 34, 53, 65, 70). I participate in Christ and his benefits. As a man who still lives here and now in time, I am nevertheless certainly and joyfully on the way to my justification in judgment (q. 52). In faith I may look forward to this judgment, knowing that the Judge who waits for me will acquit me. Faith means to accept as true, wholeheartedly to trust, what is said to us in God's Word (q. 21). Faith, then, is an *anticipation* of our status at the last judgment. I trust that God's right in relation to me, and therefore my right in relation to God, has been reestablished, although I am still in the condition and order of "sin and guilt" and must ever again confess that I am in this condition. But because I accept this *end* as true and place my confidence in it, I anticipate and look forward to it, thankful that I am on the way to it. I may already know what my sentence will be in the last judgment. In Christ it has already been spoken, even though for me the final act of judgment still lies in the future.

Question 60. **How are you righteous before God?** Only by true faith in Jesus Christ. In spite of the fact that my conscience accuses me that I have grievously sinned against all the commandments of God, and have not kept any one of them, and that I am still ever prone to all that is evil, nevertheless, God, without any merit of my own, out of pure grace, grants me the benefits of the perfect expiation of Christ, imputing to me his righteousness and holiness as if I had never committed a single sin nor had ever been sinful, having fulfilled myself all the obedience which Christ has carried out for me, if only I accept such favor with a trusting heart.

Questions 59 and 60 form a circle. To believe means *to be on the way* to meet judgment as one who *will* be justified. But in believing I am already sure of my justification; I *am* already "righteous before God." Faith is the confidence of the man called to the church of Jesus Christ. There is no private Christianity. As the final judgment is a very public affair, so also our state of justification is existence in the *communio sanctorum*.

Question 61. **Why do you say that you are righteous by faith alone?** Not because I please God by virtue of the worthiness of my faith, but because the satisfaction, righteousness, and holiness of Christ alone are my righteousness before God, and because I can accept it and make it mine in no other way than by faith alone.

Question 62. **But why cannot our good works be our righteousness before God, or at least a part of it?** Because the righteousness which can stand before the judgment of God must be absolutely perfect and wholly in conformity with the divine Law. But even our best works in this life are all imperfect and defiled with sin.

Question 63. **Will our good works merit nothing, even when it is God's purpose to reward them in this life, and in the future life as well?** This reward is not given because of merit, but out of grace.

Question 64. **But does not this teaching make people careless and sinful?** No, for it is impossible for those who are ingrafted into Christ by true faith not to bring forth the fruit of gratitude.

To what extent is faith the way to man's justification? To what extent is man's justification bound to this way? We stand here at the center of the Reformation insight, "justification through faith alone," *sola fide*. What does that mean?

Three delimitations seem necessary:

1. Faith does not justify man—not even partly—because of any remaining or newly achieved goodness of the one who believes. Faith is also not a kind of medicine which makes sick men well and thus pleasing to God (Karl Holl!). This whole idea that justification is related to something "good" in man must be rejected, and was rejected by the Reformers. It is true that faith is the action of the good creature of God. It *is* an alteration of life. But it is the action and changed life of the man who knows himself precisely as a saved man to be the sinner described in questions 5, 8, and 13. Only the man who believes in Christ knows about "sin and guilt." Faith does not justify, therefore, because the believing man is not yet or no longer a sinner (q. 60a), but *while* he is a sinner.

2. Faith does not justify a man—not even partly—because it produces a good new life of *thankfulness*. Faith does that. The believing man will certainly also do good works in faith (q. 64: ". . . it is impossible for those who are ingrafted into Christ by true faith not to bring forth the fruit of gratitude"). These good works will certainly not go unrewarded (q. 63). But if we ask ourselves what the ground of our confidence is, we will certainly not point to our "good works." We cannot stand before God with them, for the righteousness which is valid before him must be "wholly in conformity with the divine Law" (q. 62). It is always true even in our best works that "by nature I am prone to hate God and my neighbor." It is by grace and *only* by grace that we are accepted by God.

3. Faith does not justify a man—not even partly—because of a *quality* inherent in man himself. "Not because I please God by virtue of the worthiness of my faith. . . ." Faith, too, is a *human* act. In faith also we are still in the sphere of human action and reaction, and are thus involved in all the questionableness of this

sphere. And just the believing man knows that he cannot believe by himself, but that faith is the work of the Holy Spirit. Just the man who believes will give credit to God and not to himself.

Faith justifies man because the believing man trusts in the *promise* given to the *Christian church.* The church is the congregation of men who are given to know that God's plan and will for all men has been fulfilled and in Jesus Christ has reached its goal. Men who believe see that "the satisfaction, righteousness, and holiness of Christ alone are my righteousness," and that "we have him in heaven as our Advocate in the presence of the Father." The man who believes holds fast to the righteous judgment of God. Saying yes to God and stopping his grumbling, he lives in peace with God. He is one whom *God* justifies and as such *is* then justified before God. Thus in Christ the believing man also is still on the way and yet already at the goal.

It is not his faith which justifies man, but the object and content of his faith. But this object is a gift which is conferred on him. It is a benefit which the believing man can only receive, only allow to be valid, only *trust.* This attitude is the proper response to the free kindness God exercises toward us. For with this attitude God is given the honor, the gift is accepted "as if I had never commited a single sin" (q. 60c). That is the "venture of faith." "The righteous man will *live* his faith." There is a real correspondence between faith and its object. It will not occur to the believing man to boast of his faith, but he may and will accept the fact that God has been well pleased with him.

Thus *faith* and faith *alone* is the way which leads to man's justification in judgment.

16 / God's Righteousness in Baptism and the Lord's Supper

(QUESTIONS 65-68)

The eventful witnesses to God's righteous action in Jesus Christ are the acts of baptism and the Lord's Supper, in which the Christian represents and receives the confirmation of his faith, and in which therefore the church represents and receives the confirmation of its origin in Jesus Christ and its life through him.

Question 65. **Since, then, faith alone makes us share in Christ and all his benefits, where does such faith originate?** The Holy Spirit creates it in our hearts by the preaching of the holy gospel, and confirms it by the use of the holy Sacraments.

We come now to a section of the Heidelberg Catechism, "The Holy Sacraments," which is noteworthy and interesting in several respects. The introductory question 65 raises a certain problem from the very beginning. We are told here that the Holy Spirit *creates* and *confirms.* One would expect something to be said in the following questions about preaching. But this is not the case. For twenty questions the catechism speaks only of "confirmation" through the use of the holy sacraments. Where is the doctrine of the creation of faith through preaching which was all-important to the Reformers (Rom. 10:17:"Faith comes from what is heard, and what is heard comes by the preaching of Christ.")?

There is of course a simple historical explanation for this remarkable state of affairs. The interpretation of baptism and the Lord's Supper is traditionally one of the main parts of the church's catechism. At the time of the Reformation, moreover, particular care was necessary at this point because of the debate with Roman Catholicism on one side and with the Lutheran doctrine of the Supper on the other. But even when we take this into consideration, this section is still a strangely unprepared and unorganized one within the structure of the catechism. Where is the particular doctrine of the Word of God in preaching, proclamation, and instruction?

The Heidelberg Catechism connects the sacraments with the question of justifying faith: "Where does such faith originate?" The answer is that the Holy Spirit *creates* it in our hearts by preaching and *confirms* it by the use of the sacraments (cf. qq. 53, 19, 21). The catechism does not speak of an effect of the sacraments alongside preaching, much less of the possibility of their replacing preaching! The sacraments open up a new aspect of the same thing. They are a *second source* of faith which does not, however, create faith but is rather the basis for confirming faith. Faith is thus already presupposed. The sacraments are holy "signs" and "seals." This confirmation also is not a human accomplishment, but the work of the Holy Spirit. There is a divine confirmation which is no less urgent and necessary than the creation of faith.

Question 66. **What are the Sacraments?** They are visible, holy signs and seals instituted by God in order that by their use he may the more fully disclose and seal to us the promise of the gospel, namely, that because of the one sacrifice of Christ accomplished on the cross he graciously grants us the forgiveness of sins and eternal life.

The sacraments are a *particular form of proclamation*. One can of course ask whether it would not be better to avoid the concept "sacrament," since it has become a very loaded theological concept which gives rise to wrong ideas. The New Testament does not speak of "sacrament," but of "baptism" and "supper." Baptism and Lord's Supper are *acts of the church,* witnesses in the form of events to God's righteous action in Jesus Christ. I prefer the expression "eventful witnesses" to the classical language of Augustine concerning *signa visibilia invisibilis gratiae* [visible signs of invisible grace], because the concept "sign" is endangered by the tendency to debase it to mean *only* sign. We must emphasize that we are concerned here not with an empty but with a filled sign. But the concept "sign" is above all misleading because it makes possible a false contrast with *res,* a "thing" signified. We are concerned here not with a *thing* but with an *act* in which the church is involved. If we think otherwise, preaching and sacrament would be related to each other in a strangely incongruous way. As preaching is a bit of history, history in the form of *words,* so baptism and Lord's Supper are history in the form of *acts.* Preaching and sacrament belong meaningfully together.

Question 67. **Are both the Word and the Sacraments designed to direct our faith to the one sacrifice of Jesus Christ on the cross as the only ground of our salvation?** Yes, indeed, for the Holy Spirit teaches in the gospel and confirms by the holy Sacraments that our whole salvation is rooted in the one sacrifice of Christ offered for us on the cross.

1. Baptism and the Lord's Supper are not independently effective agents so that one receives their effects *ex opere operato.* Like preaching they are *mediation,* a pointing to something else, by the power of the free work of the Holy Spirit.

2. Baptism and the Lord's Supper are not, however, mediation in the sense that they mediate a special grace which is different from the grace mediated by preaching. Preaching *and* sacrament refer to the sacrifice of Jesus Christ. Baptism and Lord's Supper also have to do with God's righteous action in Jesus Christ, with his death and resurrection, with forgiveness of sin and everlasting life. No less, but also no more!

3. Baptism and the Lord's Supper do not mediate the one grace through the so-called "elements" but through the use of them in the action of the congregation.

4. This use by no means rests on a self-sufficient effect or doctrine.

In other words, we are concerned here with *confirmations* of the faith created through preaching. The sacraments are not private affairs; they belong to the church. The faith of the individual and the faith of the gathered congregation is to be confirmed. It is to be made joyful and sure of itself by a new confirmation. Baptism (the *sacramentum initiationis,* sacrament of initiation) confirms the *origin* of faith, its past establishment. The Lord's Supper (the *sacramentum nutritionis,* sacrament of nourishment), confirms the *endurance* of faith, its coming renewal. Baptism and Supper thus mark off the room in which Christian faith may live.

Faith does not rest on itself, but on God's action. The Holy Spirit creates faith through preaching. The same Holy Spirit confirms the reality of the righteous action of God, and therefore the reality of our faith, through the actions which precede (baptism) and follow (Supper) preaching. Exactly as in preaching, the believing congregation and the believing individual are involved in this action as both subject and object, both acting and receiving. As in the creation of faith, so in this confirmation of faith we have to do with the work of the Holy Spirit. Only he, only God himself, can make these actions to be "eventful witnesses." In themselves, baptism and Lord's Supper are creaturely, human practices like others. How could they be effective in and through themselves? The Holy Spirit, God himself, confirms his reality for us through these actions. He establishes and he renews the church. He is not bound to these forms of the church's words and actions, but he works in them also. There is no point in valuing preaching and sacraments differently. What we can say is that because the sacraments have the form of events and are not only a repetition of preaching, they are given to us "the more fully to disclose and seal to us the promise of the gospel" (cf. q. 66). In celebrating baptism and the Lord's Supper, the congregation represents and receives the confirmation of faith through the Holy Spirit. The sacraments are "instituted by God" for just this purpose, and it is only of them that we can say this.

Question 68. **How many Sacraments has Christ instituted in the New Testament?** Two, holy Baptism and the holy Supper.

Baptism and Lord's Supper are instituted in and with the church. Whoever thinks he can do without them, whoever wants to be all too pious here (all varieties of so-called mysticism consider the sacraments superfluous)—let him see whether he really can dispense with the question of the *confirmation* of his faith, or whether he does not despise a gift which he needs and which he can only thankfully accept.

17 / *The Establishment of Faith in the Witness of Baptism*

(QUESTIONS 69-74)

Baptism is the action which eventfully bears witness to Christians that they have already entered into the fellowship of the death of Jesus Christ and may therefore once and for all be certain of their faith and in faith of the forgiveness of their sins.

Baptism is the answer (or rather one form of the answer) to the question: Am I rightly called *a Christian?* (cf. q. 32). I am one; I am a member of Christ and his church (q. 54); in faith I share in the benefits of the righteous action of God. Because I participate through faith in the anointing of Christ, I am a Christian. But do I really *believe?* Am I on the way to meet judgment by way of my justification (qq. 59-64)? That is not self-evident. In fact everything we hear at the beginning of question 60 speaks *against* it. If that is true, if precisely in faith I must confess that it is true, then how is it with my faith? It understands the promise, but does it also lay hold of that promise? When the catechism speaks of the confirmation of faith, it intends to overcome this doubt which can express itself in a thousand forms of greater and smaller qualms, this question which may be very serious or not serious at all. This confirmation is only possible by means of the *event* of a new gift of the Word of God, by a new reception of the Holy Spirit. As manna can fall only from heaven every day, but as it does in fact fall and is just enough for the next part of the way, so also faith can only be given to us ever afresh.

Everything is completed: that is what we may hold on to. That is the content of this event which lies between the sigh *Veni creator Spiritus!* [Come, Creator Spirit] and thankful joy over the fact that the righteous may *live* his faith. What you need *is* there. You *are* a Christian. You *are* on the way to meet judgment by way of justification. You are in the fellowship of the death of Christ, and you may be sure of your faith now and always. Christ died and rose again *for you also.* That is the confirmation of our faith.

But am I really only saying that to myself? Am I only preaching to myself and saying amen to myself? No. I am told in the eventful witness of my *baptism* that all this holds good for me. I may now exist as one to whom it has been said. It is just as true as my bodily existence (much more really true). I have been baptized and placed in the fellowship of the body of Christ. My faith is not self-founded. It is an objective, confirmed faith because it rests on this objective foundation. That is what my baptism attests to me.

Question 69. **How does holy Baptism remind and assure you that the one sacrifice of Christ on the cross avails for you?** In this way: Christ has instituted this external washing with water and by it has promised that I am as certainly washed with his blood and Spirit from the uncleanness of my soul and from all my sins, as I am washed externally with water which is used to remove the dirt from my body.

Question 70. **What does it mean to be washed with the blood and Spirit of Christ?** It means to have the forgiveness of sins from God, through grace, for the sake of Christ's blood which he shed for us in his sacrifice on the cross, and also to be renewed by the Holy Spirit and sanctified as members of Christ, so that we may more and more die unto sin and live in a consecrated and blameless way.

Baptism is a washing (Titus 3:5), a washing away (Acts 22:16). Romans 6:4, a text not mentioned in the catechism, describes baptism as immersion in water which symbolizes death, as a dying of man. This immersion is the *homoioma,* image, of the death of Christ. It says that when Jesus Christ died and was buried, my old self was also buried in and with him, so that I might begin to live as a new self. I, the subject of my sinful existence, died then. And as a sign of this I am included in this image of his death: I am baptized. As an action, this *homoioma* is an event in my life which testifies to me that I am set apart to be a member of Christ. I am the man to whom grace is not only promised but also given. I can live by that. Baptism does not "effect" this, but it does bear witness to it.

This event, this washing away, takes place in my life: *Baptizatus sum!* I have been baptized! And if that is true, then what this washing attests is also true and real—my rebirth effected by the Holy Spirit: *Renatus sum:* I am renewed. Question 70 speaks of this "renewal."

Question 71. **Where has Christ promised that we are as certainly washed with his blood and Spirit as with the water of baptism?** In the institution of Baptism which runs thus: "Go therefore and make disciples of all nations, baptizing them in the name of the Father, and of the Son and of the Holy Spirit." "He who believes and is baptized will be saved; but he who does not believe will be condemned." This promise is also repeated where the Scriptures call baptism "the water of rebirth" and the washing away of sins.

To make this connection between baptism and new birth is not just a nice custom. It is based on the promise of Christ in his institution of baptism in Matthew 28:19. I would suggest myself that the New Testament institution of baptism ought to be sought not in this disputed passage but in Jesus' baptism in the Jordan. It is there that we ought to look when we are baptized in his name. His baptism is the *homoioma* of his death in his own life, the earliest beginning of his solidarity with sinful men. We are baptized into the death of Christ. Engravings of the baptism of Christ in the Jordan are sometimes found on the bottom of old baptismal chalices. This is a graphic description of the fact of the matter.

Question 72. **Does merely the outward washing with water itself wash away sins?** No; for only the blood of Jesus Christ and the Holy Spirit cleanse us from all sins.

Question 73. **Then why does the Holy Spirit call baptism the water of rebirth and the washing away of sins?** God does not speak in this way except for a strong reason. Not only does he teach us by baptism that just as the dirt of the body is taken away by water, so our sins are removed by the blood and Spirit of Christ; but more important still, by the divine pledge and sign he wishes to assure us that we are just as truly washed from our sins spiritually as our bodies are washed with water.

These two questions deal with the relation between the sacramental act and what it signifies. The meaning and reality of baptism consist in this relation between water baptism and new birth, in baptism's real character as eventful witness, in the effective *significare* in which the two events are both *two* (q. 72) and yet *one* (q. 73). It is obviously God who establishes this relation. Baptism cannot become a subject; it does not "do" anything. But the Holy Spirit does something through baptism! If we enter into the argument over terminology as it was carried on with regard to the doctrine of baptism in the sixteenth century, we must say that of course we are concerned here with a *significare,* with the giving of a sign. An earthly element is used here. But it is an effective *significare,* a sign which really indicates something (cf. q. 79: Christ does not speak in this way except for a strong reason). This unity must be understood as an *unio sacramentalis,* sacramental union: Just as surely as I have been baptized, so certainly is it also real that I have entered into fellowship with Christ, that I have forgiveness of my sins in his death, that I really believe and may once and for all depend on the fact that

I believe, that I have been set on this way by God. No further word is necessary, because this *action,* this *event* which has happened once for all in our existence, bears witness that all this is true. Baptism is really not only a further bit of preaching and instruction. The questionable thing about the Augustinian expression *verbum visibile* is that it could be misunderstood in this way. Baptism and the Lord's Supper do also proclaim something, but they are "not only" proclamation; ". . . more important still, by the divine pledge and sign he wishes to *assure* us. . . ." We cannot overlook this "not only . . . but more important still." We stand in the sphere of faith and thus of the Word of God, and baptism is of course nothing other than a form of the Word of God. But just in its particular form it becomes an assurance that one can cling to. In view of my baptism it can no longer be a problem for me whether I can and may believe. All such problems are childish on this basis. Baptism simply attests to me: I *am* a believer.

Question 74. **Are infants also to be baptized?** Yes, because they, as well as their parents, are included in the covenant and belong to the people of God. Since both redemption from sin through the blood of Christ and the gift of faith from the Holy Spirit are promised to these children no less than to their parents, infants are also by baptism, as a sign of the covenant, to be incorporated into the Christian church and distinguished from the children of unbelievers. This was done in the Old Covenant by circumcision. In the New Covenant baptism has been instituted to take its place.

This question comes as a surprise. We have heard that baptism is the confirmation or establishment of faith by the assurance of its origin in the blood and Spirit of Jesus Christ. That presupposes a *believing* man who *confesses* his faith and *desires* to be baptized. And now all of a sudden, in clear contradiction to what has been said before, the catechism speaks of the baptism of *infants.* Baptism is handled in this unexpected and unfounded way in all classical Protestant theology, even in Calvin. All the previously discussed constitutive marks of baptism (especially the faith of the baptized) are suddenly ignored. One may not assume that babies believe. Is the screaming baby proof that despite his opposition the sinner is grasped by the Holy Spirit? Is faith mediated to him by baptism? Or does the faith of others take his place —the faith of the parents or godparents, perhaps, or of the congregation? Are we concerned here not with the faith of the baptized at all, but with a *representative* faith? But how is all that related to what has previously been taught about baptism?

Question 74 makes three points concerning infant baptism which as such are correct.

1. It is correct that children as well as adults belong to the *covenant of God* and that the promise of the Holy Spirit is given to both. But that does not mean that those who do not believe and thus cannot bear witness to their faith belong to the *church*. Can a living member of the church be only the object of the faith of *others?* Or does one belong to the church just because he is the child of a Christian family?

2. It is correct that children of believers are to be distinguished from other children. See 1 Corinthians 7:14! They are "holy." But again that does not mean that they are members of the church. It only means that they are distinguished insofar as a special offer is extended to them through Christian parents. But this still does not say that these children ought to be baptized.

3. It is correct that baptism replaces circumcision. This argument has always played an important part in the Reformed church. In the Dutch church one speaks of a covenant which God made not with the *church* but with Christian *nations*. If we expand this ideology, we arrive at the concept of the "Christian West." World political aspects are opened up! But is the church really to be identified with this *Corpus christianum,* "Christian society"? Everything depends on this question. Is not that which distinguished Israel from other nations (the distinction symbolized by circumcision) the fact that from this nation the *One* should come? And is not the history of this nation ended after that was fulfilled and he has come? In what sense after that can we still speak of holy nations? Are not Israel and the church two different things, and is one not accepted into the community of the new covenant on the basis of *faith?* There is no doubt that

Israel is constituted on the basis of family and nation. But the congregation of the children of God are not born by the will of man; they are called by the Word out of all nations. One of the many errors of church history is that at this point a Jewish conception could be preserved and one could speak of Christian nations. The church is no longer Israel, and Israel was not yet the church, although it is true that the covenant of God has this double form. But this means that the argument for infant baptism from circumcision is not valid. We can only say that in both cases we are dealing with *signs of the covenant,* but signs of a different kind. This is further proved by the fact that only male Israelites were circumcised, whereas also girls are baptized!

Another reason for infant baptism is often cited which the Heidelberg Catechism does not mention: namely, that precisely the baptism of the immature is a wonderful sign of prevenient grace. The Reformers made no use of this argument, and we may say that it could be convincing only if the justification for infant baptism were already proved.

The real reason for the persistent adherence to infant baptism is quite simply the fact that without it the church would suddenly be in a remarkably embarrassing position. Every individual would then have to decide whether he wanted to be a Christian. But how many Christians would there be in that case? The whole concept of a national church (or national religion) would be shaken. That must not happen; and so one proposes argument upon argument for infant baptism and yet cannot speak convincingly because fundamentally he has a bad conscience. The introduction of adult baptism in itself would of course not reform the church which needs reforming. The adherence to infant baptism is only one—a very important one—of many symptoms that the church is not alive and bold, that it is afraid to walk on the water like Peter to meet the Lord, that it therefore does not seek a sure foundation but only deceptive props.

The *consequence* of this adherence to infant baptism is the devaluation of baptism by so-called *confirmation,* in which baptism is supposed to be confirmed by faith, in which therefore the confession and desire which ought to precede baptism are supposed to be made up for later. Fifteen years later one is supposed to confirm his faith. This procedure is impossible. But it cannot be avoided so long as we hòld to infant baptism, which is indeed incomplete without this subsequent confirmation.

Another consequence is necessarily the formation of a *mass church,* the Christian character of which is never examined at all, a church which therefore cannot realize the comfort that comes from having been baptized. Under these circumstances, one need not be surprised at the stream of indifference and secularism which flows through our church.

All this is not to say that baptism as it has been practiced for centuries has not been true baptism. It remains baptism, whatever the practice may be. We are concerned here only with a question of *order.* But the question of infant baptism which has been raised anew today does call us to fresh reflection about the right order of its administration.

18 / The Renewal of Faith in the Witness of the Lord's Supper

(QUESTIONS 75-80)

The Lord's Supper is the action which eventfully bears witness to the Christian that he will ever again be sustained in the fellowship of the resurrection of Jesus Christ and that he may therefore ever again rejoice in faith in his own resurrection.

The Lord's Supper also is an answer to a question about faith: How is it that I believe now, today, and *remain* a believer? What is the source of that standing, walking, hurrying, pursuing in faith of which the New Testament speaks? In a word, how does the *life* of faith come?

The answer is: You can and you will remain, stand, walk, live in faith, because the Holy Spirit gives you the freedom to do so. "The righteous shall live his faith" (Rom. 1:17). He will *walk* his way as the prophet Elijah, having been fed in the desert, walked forty days and forty nights to Mount Horeb by the strength of that nourishment. Man "walks" in the freedom and joy of the Holy Spirit who is sent by the risen Jesus Christ as "counterpledge" (q. 49). Christ is in heaven as "flesh of our flesh." Faith grasps this gift. In faith it happens that "by the Holy Spirit dwelling both in Christ and in us" we are "united more and more to his blessed body" (q. 76). And already in this life we walk with him in the joy of the new aeon. In faith we participate in his and therefore also in our own resurrection. Am I really all that? Do I have this faith? Can I remain, walk, stand, hasten in him?

To this question there is again only one answer: Victory over doubt is only possible through the *event* of a new gift of the Holy Spirit, new hearing of the Word, new faith. And the content of this event is: You *can* and you *will* believe because you *may*, because Jesus Christ not only died but also rose and lives for you, because therefore your faith has not only an objective foundation but also an *objective permanence*. I live my faith, then, not from my own strength but from the strength of the nourishment I receive. And it is the Lord's Supper which bears witness to this nourishment offered to us.

As "eventful witness" the Lord's Supper is the assurance and promise: You will be given food and drink. You will survive. You will exist in time for eternal life. Your faith will not cease, but will again and again be renewed. You *may* rejoice in your faith.

In the Lord's Supper this promise has the form of distributing and receiving, eating of bread and drinking of wine. Corresponding to what we said of baptism, we could say of the Supper that it is the image, the *homoioma,* of the *life* of Jesus Christ. His existence as the Risen One benefits me. I may live my own resurrection. I have received the nourishment of Elijah. In the strength of this nourishment I may walk day and night to the mountain of God. I receive the "token" of this permission given me in the

Lord's Supper. That is the comfort of the gospel which is witnessed to me in the Supper: I stand in the fellowship of the resurrection of Jesus Christ, and therefore in faith I may ever anew rejoice in my own resurrection.

Questions 75-79 are set forth and formulated as parallels to questions 69-73. Like question 74, question 80 forms a supplement.

Question 75. **How are you reminded and assured in the holy Supper that you participate in the one sacrifice of Christ on the cross and in all his benefits?** In this way: Christ has commanded me and all believers to eat of this broken bread, and to drink of this cup in remembrance of him. He has thereby promised that his body was offered and broken on the cross for me, and his blood was shed for me, as surely as I see with my eyes that the bread of the Lord is broken for me, and that the cup is shared with me. Second, he has promised that he himself as certainly feeds and nourishes my soul to everlasting life with his crucified body and shed blood as I receive from the hand of the minister and actually taste the bread and the cup of the Lord which are given to me as sure signs of the body and blood of Christ.

The promise of the Lord's Supper is here divided into a "first" and a "second."

1. "His body was offered and broken on the cross for me. . . ." This first statement speaks of the promise which I now receive and which I may look forward to: I may and I shall live my faith. The reality of the death of Christ is related to the action of the Lord's Supper. The bread is broken for *me*. The cup is given to *me*. I see that with my own eyes. The real mystery of the Lord's Supper lies in the relation between the event of the death of Christ for me and the event of the presentation of bread and wine for me. As surely as what happens in the congregation at the table of the Lord takes place, just so surely is it true and real that Christ's body is broken and his blood shed for me.

2. The second statement strengthens the first by saying that *Christ himself* feeds and nourishes me to everlasting life. And

again the physical eating and drinking is my pledge, the visible earthly form of the fact that this is true. Jesus Christ himself is present to me. More than that, I may receive him; I may feed on him; I may live through him. As surely as I receive bread and wine at the Supper, just so surely he himself feeds and nourishes me to everlasting life.

Question 76. **What does it mean to eat the crucified body of Christ and to drink his shed blood?** It is not only to embrace with a trusting heart the whole passion and death of Christ, and by it to receive the forgiveness of sins and eternal life. In addition, it is to be so united more and more to his blessed body by the Holy Spirit dwelling both in Christ and in us that, although he is in heaven and we are on earth, we are nevertheless flesh of his flesh and bone of his bone, always living and being governed by one Spirit, as the members of our bodies are governed by one soul.

The question raised here is similar to that raised concerning baptism in question 70: What does it mean to eat the crucified body of Christ and to drink his blood? Here, too, a double answer is given.

It is *not only* to embrace with a trusting heart the whole passion and death of Christ, and by it to *receive* the forgiveness of sins and everlasting life; *in addition* it is to have *objective participation* in the life of Christ, so that I am united "more and more" to his blessed body (cf. qq. 70, 123). Christ did not desert us when he rose from the dead. He lives now as man before God and with God, sitting at the right hand of the Father. And we may live with him and in him. He is the source of an objective growth: in him God's confirmation of us grows stronger, the power of his grace increases in my life. It goes with my objective fellowship with him that my life on earth is governed by it. And if every individual may grow into this unity with Christ, then he also grows together with the members of Christ's body. For the Holy Spirit is the Spirit of the church and he necessarily unites it also in objective fellowship.

That is what it means to eat the body and drink the blood of Christ. As surely as I receive and partake of the bread and wine, just so surely is all that true and real. That is the reality of the Lord's Supper.

Question 77. **Where has Christ promised that he will feed and nourish believers with his body and blood just as surely as they eat of this broken bread and drink of this cup?** In the institution of the holy Supper which reads: The Lord Jesus on the night when he was betrayed took bread, and when he had given thanks, he broke it, and said, "This is my body which is for you. Do this in remembrance of me." In the same way also the cup, after supper, saying, "This cup is the new covenant in my blood. Do this, as often as you drink it, in remembrance of me." For as often as you eat this bread and drink the cup, you proclaim the Lord's death until he comes. This promise is also repeated by the apostle Paul: When we bless "the cup of blessing," is it not a means of sharing in the blood of Christ? When we break the bread, is it not a means of sharing the body of Christ? Because there is one loaf, we, many as we are, are one body; for it is one loaf of which we all partake.

The relation established in questions 75 and 76 rests on the fact that the *Lord himself* instituted the Supper. It rests on the promise and command of *Jesus Christ.* The Supper is thus not a symbol or ecclesiastical practice instituted by men, for which meaning must be invented as an afterthought. Christ himself willed and established this relation. Nor is it just a verbal relation, for by his Word, God created the whole church and also baptism and the Lord's Supper. Wherever the Supper is celebrated, there he himself is present. And where he is present, there the relation between God's food and drink and the earthly bread and wine is real.

Question 78. **Do the bread and wine become the very body and blood of Christ?** No, for as the water in baptism is not changed into the blood of Christ, nor becomes the washing away of sins by itself, but is only a divine sign and confirmation of it, so also in the Lord's Supper the sacred bread does not become the body of Christ itself, although, in accordance with the nature and usage of sacraments, it is called the body of Christ.

Question 79. **Then why does Christ call the bread his body, and the cup his blood, or the New Covenant in his blood, and why does the apostle Paul call the Supper "a means of sharing" in the body and blood of Christ?** Christ does not speak in this way except for a strong reason. He wishes to teach us by it that as bread and wine sustain this temporal life so his crucified body and shed blood are the true food and drink of our souls for eternal life. Even more, he wishes to assure us by this visible sign and pledge that we come to share in his true body and blood through the working of the Holy Spirit as surely as we receive with our mouth these holy tokens in remembrance of him, and that all his sufferings and his death are our own as certainly as if we had ourselves suffered and rendered satisfaction in our own persons.

We must understand these questions in light of the sixteenth-century discussion. The meaning and reality of the Lord's Supper consist in the relation between *two* events: earthly eating and drinking on the one hand, and eating and drinking the body and blood of Christ in the Holy Spirit on the other. But we must not read question 78 apart from question 79. As we partake of bread and wine, we do participate through the work of the Holy Spirit in Christ's body and blood. By the work of the Holy Spirit there is a *communio* here of man with Christ. There is not just a nominal but a real connection between the bread and wine and his body and blood. The Lord's Supper is more than a doctrine. It is an *assurance* (cf. q. 73: not without "strong reason"). It is a gift which is given *me* when I not only *hear* something (though I do that also!) but *participate* in the meal to which Christ himself has called and invited me. It assures me that I am once again placed in the position of the man who in faith may hold fast, stand, walk, hasten, and pursue. Christ himself feeds and nourishes me to this end. The Supper is not just a further *word* about this event; it *demonstrates* it.

Question 80. **What difference is there between the Lord's Supper and the papal Mass?** The Lord's Supper testifies to us that we have complete forgiveness of all our sins through the one sacrifice of Jesus Christ which he himself has accomplished on the cross once for all; and that through the Holy Spirit we are incorporated into Christ, who is now in heaven with his true body at the right hand of the Father and is there to be worshiped. But the Mass teaches that the living and the dead do not have forgiveness of sins through the sufferings of Christ unless Christ is again offered for them daily by the priests; (and that Christ is bodily under the form of bread and wine and is therefore to be worshiped in them). Therefore the Mass is fundamentally a complete denial of the once for all sacrifice and passion of Jesus Christ (and as such an idolatry to be condemned).

"The Lord's Supper *testifies* to us. . . ." We must not weaken this "testifies" but understand its real meaning. Then the charge of nominalism will become groundless.

The second part of this question (on the Mass) was added in the second edition, and the Elector thought it very important that the emperor be presented with this text. Here the full wrath of the Reformation against the development of the Counter-Reformation breaks out.

There is a double denial here. First, the identification of the eventful witness with the attested event is rejected. That is, the catechism protests against the concept of the *Mass* as a repetition of the unique sacrifice of Jesus Christ and against the idea that such a repetition performed by the church is necessary to salvation. The repetition is declared to be a denial of the once for all sacrifice of the Lord. Either this sacrifice is unique or it is not the sacrifice of Jesus Christ (cf. qq. 29, 30, 67, 96).

In the second place, the catechism rejects the Roman Catholic doctrine of *transubstantiation*. That also means a forbidden identification: bread and wine become by transformation *identical* with Christ's body and blood. The catechism declares this concept, with the worship which follows from it, to be a "cursed

idolatry." To think that the sacrifice of Jesus Christ can be repeated in this way is to give it over to the control of man.
"Another Christ" appears. But it is a procedure characteristic of
Catholic thinking in general that a second center is established
alongside the real center. Beside Holy Scripture stand tradition
and the infallible teaching office of the church. Beside Christ
stand the apostle Peter and the infallible church. Beside the being of God stands the being of the creature. One knows about the
grace of God, but at the same time about a co-operation of the
creature made possible by an anticipatory grace. This dualism,
this fatal "and," becomes clearest of all in the form of Mary. Christ
and Mary—creaturely being as an analogy of divine being. Which
is the real center now? Where is the decisive authority?

We must understand this secret attack on the exclusive authority of Jesus Christ if we are to understand the angry explosion
of the Heidelberg Catechism at this point. It is a very naïve tendency of many Protestants today to think that our differences from
Catholic doctrine are insignificant and that we can find common
ground in an *Una sancta* movement. Certainly we can carry on
genuine theological conversation with Catholics. Under certain
conditions we can also pray together with them. But we must not
deceive ourselves about the fact that Catholic thinking will never
give up the structure peculiar to it. We have to decide between
"Christ alone" and "Christ and. . . ." Do they "really believe in
the only Savior Jesus"? That is the question one must ask with
the Heidelberg Catechism (q. 30). The devil prowls around like
a roaring lion even when he humbles himself and occasionally
draws in his tail!

In conclusion I must call express attention to the fact that I
have interpreted the catechism's doctrine of the Lord's Supper
in a particular way.

1. As was generally the case in the sixteenth century, the catechism relates the concepts body and blood one-sidedly to the
physical aspect of the human nature of Christ instead of relating
them to the *totus homo* and *totus Christus* (the total man and
the total Christ) as I have tried to relate them in the preceding
discussion.

2. The discussion in the sixteenth century was also one-sided in its interest in the "elements" of the Lord's Supper—as the debate over "This is . . ." and "This signifies . . ." indicates. My interpretation emphasizes by way of contrast that the "This is . . ." refers to the *whole action.* The point of the Lord's Supper is an *event:* The father of the house and his guests gather at a table; bread and wine are distributed; they eat and drink and sing praises. However this event may be related to the Passover, it is certain that the words, "This is . . .," by which Jesus points to himself, refer to his sacrifice for us. You shall be nourished and fed *through me.* From this point of view the whole debate about the Lord's Supper as it was carried on in the sixteenth century is obsolete.

3. I have emphasized the evidence in the New Testament that the Lord's Supper is to be related to the *life* of the *risen* Christ in his church. In the sixteenth century one thought of the presence of Christ too one-sidedly in terms of remembrance of the one who *has* come, and therefore in terms of Good Friday. But the Supper is an anticipation of the wedding of the Lamb and thus is to be related to the one who *does* and *will* come. Then the prayer becomes meaningful: "Come, Lord Jesus, be our guest, and bless what you have given us."

19 / *The Purification of the Church*

(QUESTIONS 81-85)

In the living church the preaching of the gospel and its eventful witness in baptism and the Lord's Supper have a healing effect. They test the faith of every individual one of its members, and therefore their common faith, both with respect to the object of faith and with respect to the character of faith as responsible life decision. In this way preaching and sacrament separate belief from unbelief.

20 / Faith as Obedience

(QUESTIONS 86-93)

A command is given just to the man who, as a living member of the Christian church, may believe that God's righteousness in Jesus Christ has already been fulfilled for him. The command is that he should live in accordance with the decision about the right of God and of man which was made in the death and resurrection of his Lord.

21 / Man Before God

(QUESTIONS 94-103)

That (and only that) human action is obedient to God's command which keeps holy the right of God established in Jesus Christ in such a way that it is limited by God's incomparability and distance but also by his glory and worthiness of worship.

22 / Man with His Neighbor

(QUESTIONS 104-112)

That (and only that) human action is obedient to God's command which keeps holy the right of man established in Jesus

Christ in such a way that it also respects human dignity, preserves and furthers human life in every form, brings honor to the relationship between man and woman, creates a real community of work and compensation, and makes human speech to be an instrument of truth.

23 / The Power of God's Command

(QUESTIONS 113-115)

The divine command claims man without reservation for God and for neighbor. In so doing it has the power to call and move him to more diligent action. In view of his insufficiency, it has the power to call and move him to faith in God's righteousness in Jesus Christ, to hope in Christ's final revelation, and to prayer for his Holy Spirit.

24 / The Mystery of Prayer

(QUESTIONS 116-119)

The work of God's righteousness and the work of man's obedience come together in the freedom given the Christian to join with Jesus Christ in calling upon the one true God, whom the Christian knows he has to thank for everything and from whom he may ask everything.

25 / *Freedom for Prayer*

(QUESTIONS 120-121)

Access to prayer is the clarity and joy given to man in Jesus Christ by which in his need and hope he may believe that the one true God is not far from him but near, not against him but for him.

26 / *Prayer for the Concerns of God*

(QUESTIONS 122-124)

In Jesus Christ, God becomes visible as the God who does not will to be without man. Therefore man is allowed and commanded in his prayer first of all and above all to participate in the fulfillment of God's plan, work, and will.

27 / *Prayer for the Concerns of Man*

(QUESTIONS 125-127)

In Jesus Christ, man becomes visible as the man who does not have to be without God. Therefore he is allowed and commanded in his prayer with equal seriousness to bring to God also his own needs and expectations.

28 / *The Hearing of Prayer*

(QUESTIONS 128-129)

To pray means to take God at his word and to call upon his righteousness which has been fulfilled in Jesus Christ and has come to us as a living Word. Such calling upon God consists in praise and thanksgiving, because God's hearing and fulfilling of our petitions is greater than our desiring, has already been granted, and in and with his Word is already on the way.

II

Introduction to the Heidelberg Catechism

Lecture given on October 4, 1938, in a course for teachers of religion on the Schauenberg, near Liestal, Switzerland. The text of the German edition is based on stenographic notes made by Pastor Rolf Eberhard, then of Bubendorf.

Introduction

It is important in studying the Heidelberg Catechism to know the purpose of this little book. Its authors, Ursinus and Olevianus, intended that it should be used in four ways: (1) It should be an instrument for teaching. (2) It should be a standard of doctrine for the teachers and preachers of the Palatinate. (3) It was divided into nine readings which were to be used in cycles in the liturgy of public worship every year. (4) It was further divided into fifty-two sections which were to be the respective themes for a sermon every Sunday afternoon of the year. The catechism is thus not a piece of isolated "theory." It is significant that even externally it stands at the middle of the order of common worship, between the formulas for baptism and the Lord's Supper. Here, between baptism and the Supper, is where one finds the "only comfort" about which the fundamental first question speaks. And here at the same time we are called to explain this comfort. We cannot separate *having* comfort from *reflecting* on it. There is no life in comfort without knowledge of this comfort, and no real knowledge of it apart from life. The catechism was written in 1563. It is a document which comes from the latter part of the Reformation. Against the beginning influence of the Counter-Reformation the moats were dug deeper, the walls built higher, the Reformed faith expressed in a more careful and coherent way. The catechism expresses especially the perception of the *Re-*

formed side of the Reformation which stemmed from *Calvin.* But Ursinus was a student of Melanchthon, and we may say that the best of the Lutheran Reformation is also included here.

The catechism says what it has to say in three parts: man's misery (his sin and guilt), man's redemption and freedom, man's gratitude and obedience. Worked into this three-part outline is a succession of apparently foreign elements which shape the content of the three parts:

> Questions 23-58: The Apostles' Creed and exposition
> Questions 66-82: Baptism and Lord's Supper with explanation
> Questions 92-118: Ten Commandments and exposition
> Questions 119-129: Lord's Prayer and exposition

These are the traditional parts of the church's instruction, the so-called articles of faith which the church has always held. The fact that the Heidelberg Catechism in its way also takes up these fundamental articles shows that the Reformation was not intended to be an innovation but precisely a *re-*formation of the ancient and permanently valid essence of the church. The catechism does of course present these fundamental articles in a particular way. The outline human misery—human redemption—human gratitude is in its simplicity an ingenious restatement of the essence of the whole Reformation.

✠

Why bother with the Heidelberg Catechism? A little historical interest is not reason enough. It is not enough that until about a hundred years ago the catechism was used in church and school in Switzerland also. A historical argument is even less convincing in light of the fact that for the past hundred years the value of the catechism has been questioned from all sides (not least of all from the side of modern pedagogy) and finally laid aside. But it is becoming clear just in our time that what the Heidelberg Catechism once represented cannot be destroyed by a short century of rejection. In any case it is and remains a classical document of the faith of the church which was reformed according to God's Word. This document deserves at least a respectful hearing. It is not of course an authority to be acknowledged without reservation. The Reformed Church knows only the one authority of Holy Scripture. But alongside (or better: under) Scripture there is a *legitimate witness* to Scripture. That is what the Heidelberg Catechism intends to be.

✠

What is the faith of the church reformed according to God's Word? More recent catechetical literature begins with the question, Who is God? Or more often, Who is man? Or perhaps with the question of truth. The Heidelberg Catechism does not seem to know these questions. It begins by asking, "What is your only comfort, in life and in death?"

This question presupposes (1) that man needs comfort, (2) that there is such comfort in life and in death—*one* such comfort, (3) that there are men who can answer this first question. In the Bible, and from that source also in the catechism, comfort has a more comprehensive and more powerful meaning that we usually associate with this word. Here comfort does not mean just a little tranquilization and assurance. It means exhortation and challenge. With the encouragement of comfort we are set on our feet, and comfort is given to us as those who have been set on our feet. *The content of Christian doctrine is that it gives this comfort.* Everything else one could ask about at the beginning of Christian doctrine is included in this fact, in the event of this comfort. Who is God? He who comforts us. Who is man? He who is comforted. What is truth? The comfort given man from God. Every other question is thereby answered. The church in 1563 questioned and answered in this concentrated way. Our thinking today is much more scattered. In order to understand the witness of the Heidelberg Catechism we must therefore first of all place ourselves in the framework of this concentrated thought.

The first question and answer give rise to three questions which are determinative for the exposition of the Heidelberg Catechism:

(1) Who is the Comforter?

(2) Who is the man who is comforted?

(3) How is this comfort given? In what does it consist?

These questions are the three lines of thought which will lead us through the whole catechism. But before we take up the first of these, and without anticipating the third, we must say this: The essence of the comfort meant here, our actually being comforted, lies in the fact that according to question 1 a *situation* is established which comforts and exhorts, challenges and strengthens. This situation is that *I belong not to myself but to my faithful Savior, Jesus Christ.* All further statements in question 1 are relative clauses added to this subject, "my faithful Savior, Jesus Christ": ". . . who has fully paid for all my sins . . . completely freed me . . . protects me . . . assures me . . . makes me wholeheartedly willing and ready from now on to live for him." These are all statements about Jesus Christ. They concern me because he acts for me. The whole content of the catechism is to be understood as an explanation of this He-I relationship. I am included in what is said here because he acts for me. I am comforted because of my faithful Savior, Jesus Christ. Everything is included in this name.

1 / Who Is the Comforter?

This is the central question.

Question 18 answers: "Our Lord Jesus Christ, who is freely given to us for complete redemption and righteousness." This does not mean only that redemption and righteousness come *through* Jesus Christ, but that Jesus Christ is *himself* redemption (a word which presupposes an imprisonment) and righteousness. He is *complete redemption:* nothing is left for us ourselves or others to finish up. He is *righteousness:* that means a condition which makes right. Jesus Christ *is* this condition, and *as such* he is the Comforter.

Question 19 explains that we know this from the Old and New Testaments. Because they tell us this, the Old and New Testaments are gospel. What is "revealed," "proclaimed," "foreshadowed," and "fulfilled" there takes many forms, but in all these forms *this* is what is said: Jesus Christ is our redemption and righteousness. According to *question 29,* he of whom we know this through the gospel is Jesus (Savior). That he *saves* us points to the *redemption* mentioned in question 18; that we *find* salvation in him points to the *righteousness* mentioned in question 18.

Question 34 calls him our *Lord,* and referring back to question 1, explains what this means by saying that he has redeemed us *from* sin and all dominion of the devil, and bought us *for* his very own. This explanation again emphasizes redemption and righteousness.

How is it possible that there is one who *is* both? The answer is that this one can be both because he is true God and true man.

Questions 15-17 explain that it is human nature which must pay for its sin. But sinful man is totally unfit to make reparation for sin. Therefore the Comforter as true God must enter the picture so that by the power of his *deity* he can bear in his *humanity* the burden of God's wrath against sin. Man is needed if redemption is to take place; but above all, God is needed. That Jesus Christ is true God and true man is the mystery of his existence as our redemption and righteousness.

Question 35 speaks of this mystery of Christ's existence: conceived by the Holy Spirit, born of the Virgin Mary. This again clarifies the fact that Jesus Christ does not just *do* something; he is not just the instrument of God's help—*in his person he is himself this help.*

Question 25 draws what we have said into connection with the three-in-oneness of God. Redemption requires no less than the action of God himself. But God himself is present precisely in Jesus Christ.

Questions 26, 33, 120, clarify the point that we can have a child-Father relationship with God only because of the deity of Christ, the eternal Son of the eternal Father. What is naturally true of him alone becomes the truth about us for his sake, by grace. That is why the catechism speaks so exclusively in various places (i.e., qq. 29-30, 94-95). The emphasis here is only on the fact that God is known exclusively in *Christ*. It is by no means the fanaticism of the number one of the monotheistic religions.

Concerning the *work* of the comfort this one person brings, the catechism says the following:

Question 31 speaks of the *offices* of Christ (as contrasted with the personal names of Jesus). Christ means Anointed One. In the Old Testament, prophets, priests, and kings were anointed. Jesus Christ, the sum of all these anointed, *the* Anointed One, the one to whom they all pointed, unites this threefold office in himself.

After this question, the catechism has very little to say about the *prophetic* office. It emphasizes rather the *priestly* and *kingly* offices and work of Christ. And again in this context there is obvious reference to the redemption and righteousness of question 18.

The following questions speak of the priestly office of Christ (redemption): 36, 37, 44, 46, 49a, 52, 56, 60, 66, 67, 70a, 79.

The following questions speak of the kingly office of Christ (righteousness): 43, 45, 47, 49c, 50, 51, 52b, 54, 57, 58, 70b, 75b, 76b, 86, 123, 124, 127, 128.

The main interest of the Heidelberg Catechism is obviously in the second line, the kingly office, righteousness.

Jesus Christ is our Comforter because and in that he took our place before God (priestly office, redemption). He was able to do that because he was the beloved Son of the Father who became like us. But as such he does not leave us to ourselves; he has taken us in hand as his possession (kingly office, righteousness).

He accompanies with his Spirit those who have been purified by his blood. This juxtaposition of the *blood* and the *Spirit* of Christ is important and characteristic in the Heidelberg Catechism. It also points to the unity of the two things we have already encountered several times:

Blood = redemption = Jesus Christ the Priest.

Spirit = righteousness = Jesus Christ the King.

2 / Who Is Comforted?

According to question 1, the general answer to this question is: That man is comforted who no longer belongs to himself, who is driven out of the situation in which he can control and rule himself—the man who has become the property of Jesus Christ (qq. 1 and 34).

Question 53 describes the new situation of the comforted man by saying that through the Holy Spirit he is made "to share in Christ and all his benefits." We are taken into a fellowship in which everything *he* does and is applies also to us.

Question 20 speaks even more strongly when it says that the comforted man is "incorporated into him," that is, actually made a part of Christ's own self. This state of being comforted is most often described in the expression of *question 32,* "I am a member of Christ" or "I share in Christ." (Together with question 31, question 32 is one of the most important and instructive of the whole catechism.) According to question 32, the man who becomes a Christian actually becomes himself a Christ. In the strict dependence on Christ which is demanded here, question 32 says that the Christian also has "offices" corresponding to the three-fold office of Christ himself (q. 31). He himself becomes a *prophet:* ". . . so that I may confess his name." He himself becomes a *priest:* ". . . offer myself a living sacrifice of gratitude to him." He himself becomes a *king:* ". . . and fight against sin and the devil with a free and good conscience throughout this life and hereafter rule with him in eternity over all creatures."

Question 55a describes the same situation with the concept of "fellowship" (partaking) in the benefits of the person of Christ.

Question 54c says that to be a "member of Christ" (with all the consequences which have been previously named) is to be a "member of the church."

Question 76, which deals with the Lord's Supper, is the strongest statement of the unity of Christians with Christ. "To embrace with a trusting heart the whole passion and death of Christ" means that we are "flesh of his flesh and bone of his bone, always living and being governed by *one* Spirit, as the members of our bodies are governed by *one* soul." Who is comforted? The first decisive answer to this question is: the man who is not only on the way from birth to death, but on the way from baptism to Lord's Supper. But this is once again to emphasize that the name of Jesus Christ determines everything. *We are not allowed for one second to reflect on man in and of himself.* Man belongs with Jesus Christ. It is true that man is only "member" on earth,

whereas Jesus Christ the "head" is in heaven. But in this relationship of the absolute superordination of Christ and subordi-
nation of man, man is included. He is lifted up in a double sense:
he no longer exists independently, but just when he is in the hand
of his Lord he really is exalted. That is the presupposition with
which we must begin in all our thinking. We *live* in this context.
We cannot act as if Jesus Christ ceased even for a minute to be
the Prophet, Priest, and King in whom we participate.

We must not forget this when we now go on to speak of the
sin and *faith* of man as a further answer to the question, Who
is comforted? *Not one single word may be said about sin abstractly,* not one word separated from the *presupposition* about
what man is in Jesus Christ. We cannot, for instance, speak of
"man in contradiction" (or "man in revolt") in such a comfortless
way that first of all he remains where he is. And what is true concerning the sin of man is correspondingly true also concerning
the faith of man.

✞

Who is comforted? Further answer to this question must refer
again to *question 31*. The decisive statements for the catechism
here are those concerning Christ the Priest and Christ the King.
And they are related to the redemption and righteousness men-
tioned in question 18. *Two* lines run continuously through the
Heidelberg Catechism: (1) Priest—redemption—blood of Christ.
But something has happened not only *for* us but *to* and *in* us.
Therefore (2) King—righteousness—imparting of his Spirit.

In *question 70* (on baptism!) these two parts of the work of
Christ, Christ *for* us and Christ *to* and *in* us, are placed together.
But in *question 70b* the latter is further divided into two parts:
we are renewed and sanctified so that we may "more and more *die*
unto sin and *live* in a consecrated and blameless way."

Question 88 takes this contrast up again with a description of
repentance as a summary of what may and must and will happen
to man. Repentance has two parts: "the dying of the old self and
the birth of the new." Everything else the Heidelberg Catechism
has to say about man follows from this.

✝

Question 89 discusses the *dying of the old self:* "sincere sorrow over our sins and more and more to hate them and to flee from them." *I* am the subject here. I am sorry for my sins; I hate them and flee from them. But all this is true against the background of questions 70b and 43. *The cross of Christ is the beginning of this situation.* To die to sin means to be crucified with him! We do not know ourselves as sinners and we do not become sorry for our sins through self-analysis. It is rather so that *in Christ* we are *identified* as sinners and at the same time disposed of as sinners. We can speak of sin only *subsequently.* In the light of *Christ* and his action on behalf of sinners I can only be sorry for my sins, only hate them and flee from them. The cross is the *first* thing and all talk about sin can only be the *second* thing. Who we ourselves are and what the misery of man means can be seen only on the basis of the cross, where God has cared for us, taking all the misery of human existence on himself. Who are the comforted? Who are we? We are men who are miserable in our sin and guilt.

Question 5: We are men who cannot "perfectly" obey the law of God. "Not perfectly" means not at all! For according to question 62, "the righteousness which can stand before the judgment of God must be *absolutely* perfect and *wholly* in conformity with the divine law." Question 113 tells us what God's law demands of us: "That there should never enter our heart even the least inclination or thought contrary to any commandment of God, but that we should always hate sin with our whole heart and find satisfaction and joy in all righteousness." But we are prone to hate God and our neighbor (q. 5).

Question 7: Our nature is poisoned.

Question 8: We are so perverted that we are "altogether unable to do good and prone to do evil."

Question 9: Although we were created good (q. 6), by deliberate disobedience we have cheated ourselves out of the original gifts of God, so that we now stand under the wrath of God (q. 10).

Question 13: I can do nothing to change this situation. Nor can any other power in the world abolish this miserable state in which I exist. No creature can bear for me the burden of the wrath of God. I am left to depend on myself—and I am in no position to help myself.

That is the old self! My nature is spontaneously to give myself to this contradiction.

But now precisely at this point it must be said that we can reflect on these first statements of the Heidelberg Catechism only on the basis of Jesus Christ! During the last 300 years there have been those who have bemoaned the gloomy colors with which the catechism paints the picture of man's misery. Is there not after all something like a "point of contact" remaining in man, a spark which may be covered by the ashes but which is not completely extinguished?

There is no doubt that glorious things can be said about man to be set over against the first statements of the Heidelberg Catechism. There is only a single point on the basis of which these statements are true and simply self-evident: on the basis of the completed relationship of man to Jesus Christ! Man's relationship to sun and moon does indeed not reveal *that*. And the question is which relationship we want as the framework of our thinking. If we follow the catechism's line of thought, this is how we must think: Jesus Christ has acted for me! That is what it took. As a result of this event, who am I? We learn who we are from the heights of God's kindness, from the greatness of his grace, from the depth of his compassion. All these first statements of the catechism which are supposedly so horrible are not horrible at all; they are already genuine statements of great *thankfulness*.

We really need the compassion which has been shown to us. That is what these opening statements intend to tell us. They have nothing at all to do with the pessimism which one might think he finds here. They are not an abstract discussion of the "misery of man" or of the "doctrine of sin." Nothing they say is true apart from Jesus Christ.

"Sorrow over our sins," and "to hate them and to flee from them" (q. 89), can only mean *to let Christ be my body and to seek him more and more*. To be sorry for and hate and flee from sin can no longer mean a particular work. It can only mean humbly and seriously, but above all joyfully and thankfully, to let happen what *has* happened in Jesus Christ.

This is how the old self dies. *He dies from joy at the new self!* The whole "art" of the Christian life is to learn to repeat: *Thou hast borne all sin.*

Question 90 describes the birth of the new self: "Complete joy in God through Christ and a strong desire to live according to the will of God in all good works." How do we receive this? Do we have to talk ourselves into it? That would not be a real resurrection. Here, too, we must look back to the doctrine of Jesus Christ.

Question 45b tells us that as the death of the old self is the death of Christ so the resurrection of the new self is the resurrection of Christ. Therefore, because Christ is risen, I am risen *with* him. (Questions 90 and 45 go together just as 89 and 43 do.) In the strict sense, it is not I but he who is the new man. But just for that reason I cannot remain outside the new life. Because the Head does not remain in death, also the members cannot remain there.

Therefore we must ask once again: Who is the man who is comforted? Who are we? And the answer is: the *redeemed* man.

What does it mean to be redeemed? Here we run into the concept *faith*. The redeemed man is he of whom it is said in question 65 that the Holy Spirit creates faith in his heart by the preaching of the holy gospel and confirms it by the use of the holy sacraments. The Holy Spirit who creates and confirms faith is the power of the resurrection of Christ. But what is faith?

Question 21 answers that it is a knowledge by which I have a wholehearted trust (created by the Holy Spirit) that God out of sheer grace has given me forgiveness of sins, everlasting righteousness, and salvation. The new man is thus the man who accepts as true and lets it hold good that for the sake of Christ, righteousness is *given* to him. To be the new self is to be the recipient of a gift.

Question 60 (one of the central questions of the catechism) leaves no doubt that the old self is still there. But in faith I am nevertheless righteous—not because my faith is such a beautiful thing, but because my faith has *this object. Question 61* can therefore actually say that I am righteous *by* faith. Faith of course does not justify me because of the worthiness of my believing, but only because of its *goal.* That I believe in this sense, that I may look toward this goal and no longer have to look back at the old self—that is the existence of the new self.

Question 62: Even our best works are all imperfect and defiled with sin.

Question 63: Our good works merit nothing.

Question 81: Those who are displeased with themselves for their sins are to come to the table of the Lord.

All these statements strongly underline the fact that only on the basis of its goal is faith the existence of the new self.

But just when it is seen this way, this existence can and may be lived—*prayerfully* lived.

Question 117 explains that it is just in prayer that we take seriously our need and our evil condition, and humble ourselves before the majesty of God.

Question 115 says that in this new existence everything can only lead us to "more eagerly seek forgiveness of sins and righteousness in Christ." In this singleness of purpose we are righteous before God. *We are righteous before God in looking completely away from ourselves to the "foreign" righteousness of Jesus Christ.* The result of the new existence is not that something praiseworthy is found in man. *Christ* is to be praised! His light, the light of his death and resurrection, falls on *us.* The power of *his* blood and *his* Spirit is *effective* for us. It places us before God as we ought to stand before him.

3 / How Is Comfort Given?
In What Does It Consist?

In answering this question we must remember that the whole emphasis of the Heidelberg Catechism lies in its statements about the Comforter. From him there falls a light on those who are comforted. This light *as such* is the theme of this third section.

✠

We are comforted in that the *Comforter* (true God and true man, Priest and King) is with *us* (sinners who may have faith). *That* is comfort. More is not needed. Comfort is the presence of the Comforter.

✠

This third aspect of the nature of comfort is expressed in the three verbal clauses of question 1b (the question which determines the course of the whole catechism): "he *protects me* . . . therefore, by his Holy Spirit, he also *assures me of eternal life,* and *makes me wholeheartedly willing and ready* from now on to live *for him.*"

✠

A. *"He protects me."* That is, he guards, preserves, provides, so that nothing can happen to me. It is not self-evident that we are so protected. Questions 10-14 say clearly enough that by himself man cannot stand but can only fall. He stands under God's wrath and punishment. If man is not struck by this wrath and punishment, it is only because of the reality of this protection.

Question 26, which can be understood in its full significance only when it is connected with what the catechism says about man's sin and guilt, calls God *for the sake of Christ his Son my God and my Father.* He confronts me in such a way that I may accept everything, including evil, from his hand. Because it comes from him (not from chance or fate), it works in one way or another for my best interests. As we had to warn against confusing the catechism's statements about man's sinfulness with pessimism, so now we must warn against thinking of optimism.

Question 28, referring to Romans 8:23 ff., says that for the sake of Jesus Christ we are placed in the context of God's love in such a way that no creature can separate us from it. By God's invitation we may live, have confidence, be thankful. If there is a command of God in this context, according to *question 118* it is to ask of God "all things necessary for soul and body." We are to *fear* God, and we are also called to place our *confidence* in him: *both* are grounded in the certainty that "God *has become* our Father *through Christ"* (q. 120).

✠

B. *"Therefore, by his Holy Spirit, he also assures me of eternal life."* That is, he puts under our feet new ground on which we can confidently walk; ground from which we can catch sight of an eternal, true, indestructible life; where, since God is with us, we may participate in God's own true life. From a second point of view *that* is the comfort with which we are comforted. In what does it consist?

Question 54 points to the church. It is the Holy Spirit who assures me of eternal life. But the work of the Spirit takes place in a special way *in the church:* ". . . from among the whole human race, the Son of God, by his Spirit and his Word, gathers, protects, and preserves for himself . . . a congregation chosen for eternal life." By his Spirit the Son adds us to this congregation, so that the gospel may take effect. "To be comforted" thus means *election, gift, grace.* It means first of all a calling out, a choosing, of each individual—but at the same time the calling out to membership in this group, the church.

Why so? What has the church to do with the Holy Spirit and eternal life? Just this: there is where the gospel is found and where it prevails (q. 19).

Question 19: It is only from the gospel that I know of this comfort.

Question 67: In the gospel the Holy Spirit teaches, and in the sacraments he confirms, my comfort in the sacrifice of Christ.

Question 65: By the preaching of the gospel and the use of the sacraments the Holy Spirit works *faith* in our hearts.

Question 21: Through faith this assurance (q. 1) becomes real to us.

How does faith help?

Question 59 answers that it assures me that I am righteous before God and *an heir of eternal life.* I may therefore rejoice in my life as a true life. Why?

Question 60 says that it is because faith is a real acceptance of God's kindness—the forgiveness of sins, the imputed righteousness and holiness of Christ. If I accept God's favor, then:

Question 44: "... in my severest tribulations I may be *assured* that Christ my Lord has redeemed me from hellish anxieties and torments." Secretly or openly I am always in the midst of tribulation. But the meaning of comfort is that all that has already been dealt with.

Questions 52, 57, and 58 expressly use the key word *comfort.* These questions deal with my future, including death. Facing the future, I may know that Jesus Christ is for me.

Question 52: The Judge is my friend.

Question 58: In *this* future I will praise God forever.

But faith is not just a means by which one day we will get something different and better; in faith it is all present here and now.

Question 49: We have God's Spirit as a counterpledge. Because faith is the work of the Holy Spirit, in faith eternal life is already present.

Question 53b (strongly underlined by 53a): The difference between present and future is not a difference of *content* but only one of *form.* Now we believe what *then* will be revealed. As God is one and the same, so what we have now in faith and what is yet to come are not two different things. The Holy Spirit who assures us of eternal life is not some little ghost but this one Spirit, God himself.

✠

C. He *"makes me wholeheartedly willing and ready from now on to live for him."*

We have looked at two lines of thought in the Heidelberg Catechism: Jesus Christ the Priest—redemption—blood; and Jesus Christ the King—righteousness—Spirit. Now the catechism goes on to clarify something which could still separate us from the second line: *me, willing, ready, to live.* Words and concepts which refer to me myself. I cannot simply observe this heavenly-earthly drama of Christ's priestly and kingly work. I myself am involved. If it could be simply observed, this work would no longer be what it is. The last expressions of question 1 make unmistakably clear how immediately we are concerned.

We have already sensed this immediate involvement as we looked at *questions 88-90* with the question concerning who is comforted. We would quite simply not have heard the message of the one comfort if nothing followed this dying and rising. If we could previously speak of *faith* as that which summarizes everything, we must now take into consideration the fact that faith is always *my* faith or *your* faith. When faith is there, *we* are there.

Question 64, therefore, answers the question whether such teaching (justification through faith) does not make us careless and sinful with a flat "impossible!" It does not say that one must understand this teaching properly, or that this or that must be supplemented. It says simply "impossible!" It would not be *this* teaching if those who are comforted did not bring forth the fruit of thankfulness. The catechism has to this point always spoken of those ingrafted into Christ. Such people really cannot be careless and sinful.

Questions 31 and 32 tell us why question 64 can speak this "impossible" so confidently. To the prophetic office of Christ corresponds our "confessing his name"; to his priestly office corresponds our offering ourselves "a living sacrifice of gratitude to him"; to his kingly office corresponds our "fighting against sin and the devil with a free and good conscience." This connection between Christ and the Christian, effected by faith, cannot be broken. It is not so that I believe in Jesus Christ and then confess, thank, fight. Believing is not something different from these things. Faith itself is our participation in Christ and thus in his action. *Faith involves us in this action.* If we are not involved in this *action,* we do not *believe.* One has falsified the Christian teaching as soon as he separates faith from life. There is no such thing as a believing which is not confessing, thanking, fighting. There is no life of confessing, thanking, and fighting which is not the life of faith. *In Jesus Christ there is no such separation.* Therefore question 64 of the catechism says confidently: *impossible!*

✠

Question 86 summarizes the content of the first and second parts of the catechism ("Since we are redeemed from our sins. . .") and then asks: "Why must we do good works?" The answer is as simple as it is precise: because we have no other alternative but to be thankful. Nothing is left of our existence but what exists in Christ. The old is past; the realization of the new is not within our power. No other possibility remains except for us to be thankful. What does that mean?

Since we *may* live from God's grace, we *do* live from it. Thankfulness and grace correspond to each other. *Thankfulness is the attitude of the man who lives by grace and does not plunge again into the abyss from which he has been saved.*

Question 87 says the same thing negatively: "Can those who do not turn to God from their ungrateful, impenitent life be saved?" *"Certainly not"* (corresponding to the "impossible" of q. 64). Why not? Because God does not accept sinners? No; Jesus Christ *died* just for sinners. But he died for *those* sinners who *in* their sinfulness have become thankful, who are sorry for their sin and hate it and flee from it (q. 89), who have joy in God and a strong desire to live according to the will of God (q. 90). Not to be *sorry* for my sin means that I do not accept the *love* which died for me in my sin.

It is noteworthy how careful and restrained is the formulation of these statements of the catechism about the life of thankful obedience. It speaks only of being sorry for our sins. No catalogue of virtues is given. It is enough that this life is the work of grace and that good works proceed from it alone. Only that is required, but that *is* required. The question whether I *can* do even this little thing is quite pointless. Because *that* is required of me, nothing is asked of me except that I *be one who is redeemed!*

It is true that "even our best works in this life are all imperfect and defiled with sin" (q. 62), and that even those who are converted to God "cannot keep his commandments perfectly" (q. 114). We have no proof of our thankfulness to offer. We have no works of thankfulness to show off. Whoever thinks he has something to show off here has not understood what it means to live from grace. But the same question 114 also says that we should not let the matter end with not fulfilling the law. Just this question speaks of a "small beginning in obedience" and of a "serious purpose to conform not only to some, but to all the commandments of God." But once again the meaning of this thankfulness very concretely required of us can only be that "not we ourselves but thy holy name may be glorified forever" (q. 128). There are, of course, *works* of thankfulness. But what are they?

Question 91 answers clearly enough: "Only those which are done out of true faith, in accordance with the Law of God, and for his glory, and not those based on our own opinion or on the traditions of men."

The importance of the concept of thankfulness in the Heidelberg Catechism is indicated by the fact that it occurs continuously throughout the whole work (qq. 28, 32, 43, 64, 86).

Question 116 shows what this thankfulness *means* as that reception of grace which is automatically new life. Here it is said that *prayer* is the chief part of gratitude. This again points to the connection between creed and deed, theory and practice. When I really pray, I prove just in this way the genuineness of my fear of God and confidence in him.

Question 122: When I pray, "Hallowed be thy name," I *begin* to know God rightly, to hallow, glorify, and praise him. If I did not pray this way, I would not really be praying.

Question 123: When I pray, "Thy kingdom come," I *am* willing and ready to affirm the church of Jesus Christ as the dawn of his kingdom.

Question 124: When I pray, "Thy will be done," I *subject* myself to the will of God and *renounce* my will.

Question 125: When I pray, "Give us this day our daily bread," I *acknowledge* God as the only source of all that is good.

Question 126: When I pray, "Forgive us our debts," I *humble* myself before God and put myself in a position to forgive my neighbor.

Question 127: When I pray, "Lead us not into temptation," I *am* confident of God's help.

In view of this prayer, who could still speak of careless and sinful people? Just this prayer is an alarm and call to battle which summons man to the *work* which follows precisely from prayer. In depending entirely on grace, in actually *praying* for it, we submit ourselves to the commandments which once again (qq. 94 ff.) do not come from man but only and completely from *God*.

✠

Why this thankfulness? Why good works? Why Christian life?

Question 86 answers quite clearly. Not "Because we . . ." but "Because Christ. . . !" *Christ is the subject of this thankfulness, of good works and the Christian life!*

Question 32 speaks of *me! But of me insofar as I share in Christ!* It is in the closed circle of this He-I relationship that *this* thankfulness, *these* good works, the *Christian* life, take place. I am involved in his prophetic, priestly, and kingly office and now on my side I confess his name, offer my life as a sacrifice of thanksgiving, with free conscience fight against sin and the devil.

But I am involved, as *question 81* says, only as one who is displeased with myself for my sins but nevertheless trusts that these sins have been forgiven for Christ's sake. We must not (in the name of a "Christian life," for instance) make anything else of this thankfulness. Grace would then become *judgment* (q. 81b)!

✠

Question 115 says that the Ten Commandments are to be preached *first* that we may become aware of our sinfulness, and *second,* that we may diligently apply ourselves, and pray to God for the Holy Spirit who renews us. This *first* and *second* belong together. Without either we would not be the *believing sinners* we must and may confess ourselves to be.

The conclusion of the Heidelberg Catechism clarifies what its overall purpose is: *that thy holy name may be glorified forever* (q. 128). And question 129 says: "This shall truly and certainly be. For my prayer is much more certainly heard by God than I am persuaded in my heart that I desire such things from him."

The greatness of God is always superior to even the best (i.e., prayer) which can be said of man!